THE
BILLION DOLLAR
SOLUTION

THE
BILLION DOLLAR
SOLUTION

SECRETS OF PROCHAIN
PROJECT MANAGEMENT

ROBERT C. NEWBOLD

ProChain Press

The following are trademarks of ProChain Solutions, Inc.: task engagement, RACER, ProChain Project Management, PPM Checklist Survey, PPM Expert Certification, PPM Communication Plan, Cycle of Results, CORE, and impact chain.

The following are registered trademarks of ProChain Solutions, Inc.: ProChain, ProChain Solutions, and ProChain Enterprise.

PMBOK is a registered trademark of the Project Management Institute.

Microsoft is a registered trademark of the Microsoft Corporation.

Appendix B, in substantially the same form, was first published in the Cutter IT Journal, March 2003, under the title "Bridging the Reality Gap."

Publisher's Cataloging in Publication
(Provided by Quality Books, Inc.)

Newbold, Robert C. (Robert Clinton), 1954–
The billion dollar solution : secrets of ProChain project management / Robert C. Newbold.
p. cm.
Includes bibliographical references and index.
LCCN 2008937682
Hardcover: ISBN-13: 978-1-934979-05-1
ISBN-10: 1-934979-05-8
E-book: ISBN-13: 978-1-934979-06-8
ISBN-10: 1-934979-06-6

1. Project management. I. Title.

HD69.P75N483 2008   658.4'04
                          QBI08-600260

CONTENTS

ACKNOWLEDGEMENTS

This book is ongoing work. It has involved many people over many years and thus there are many who deserve credit.

None of this would be real without the help of the many clients we've worked with over the years who have lent their intelligence, expertise, and passion not only to improving their companies but to helping develop and refine the ProChain methodology. Without them, it would all be theory. Rather than list the contributions or achievements of specific companies and individuals, which in many cases would violate their confidentiality, it's better to give a heartfelt, inclusive "thank you."

This is also a work of the whole ProChain consulting organization, past and present. The evolution of the ProChain concepts has in many ways been driven by the men and women whose on-the-ground interactions with clients have informed and pushed our growth and learning. Every chapter in this book has been touched profoundly by the knowledge, brainpower, and years of experience of our consultants. It has been and continues to be a great and exciting journey.

Thanks to those many non-ProChain consultants whose successes—and failures—we have been permitted to learn from. This includes not only those who implement solutions based on critical chain scheduling techniques, but more generally those concerned with management problems and those who have documented their ideas and efforts. There is a great deal of valuable literature out there, and in many cases our job has been to organize, sift, and synthesize rather than to invent.

Editors Sharon Goldinger at PeopleSpeak and Ron Kenner at RKedit, along with designer Michael Rohani at RD Studio, deserve thanks for helping to ensure—at least as far as I would let them—that the book is both readable and presentable.

And last but certainly not least, many thanks to the many people who have reviewed this book and provided thoughtful comments, including Peter Irwin, Patrick Ryan, Allen Warren, Fred Wiersema, and of course my colleagues at ProChain Solutions.

PREFACE

Critical chain project scheduling is a technology that has the power to improve dramatically the performance of projects of all types in companies of all sizes. We founded ProChain Solutions in 1996 to learn more about that technology and to help organizations apply it effectively.

To make critical chain technology feasible in the complex world of project management, in 1997 we released ProChain Project Scheduling, the first commercially available software to support critical chain scheduling.

As we discovered the true power of critical chain scheduling, we wanted to tell people about it. That was the purpose of my first book, *Project Management in the Fast Lane.*[1]

Most of today's popular improvement approaches, such as Lean, Six Sigma, and Theory of Constraints, derive their true power through helping people improve the way they work together. These approaches facilitate organizational synchronization. No matter how interesting you find the tools associated with these approaches, the real challenges to adoption—and the greatest opportunities for improved performance—involve the people of an organization: the way they work together and the structures they've created.

In the twelve years since ProChain Solutions was founded, we've learned a great deal about the practical ramifications of implementing the critical chain technology. We've addressed the implementation challenges and opportunities through the development of what we call ProChain Project Management or "PPM," an integrated methodology that combines tools such as critical chain scheduling with processes for applying and implementing those tools.

While the PPM methodology involves scheduling and critical chain, this is neither a scheduling book nor a guide to project management. Many disciplines are involved in project management and this kind of book most assuredly can not cover them all. Instead, I describe our billion-dollar solution for scheduling, tracking, and managing projects—an approach that can be adapted to dramatically improve project management's impact in just about any organization. Based on exceptional real-world results in some of the world's best-known companies, we have become convinced that the PPM methodology will transform entire industries.

This book is for people at all levels who want to understand how to improve the performance of their project organizations, whether they are managing tasks, projects, portfolios of projects, or entire companies. It's for those who want a billion-dollar solution.

INTRODUCTION

Take a dollar bill out of your wallet. Light a match and set the dollar on fire. Examine your feelings as you did that. Were you uncomfortable?

Now go to your bank, withdraw a billion dollars and, over the course of the next year, burn them all. Bring a big briefcase: all those bills, placed end-to-end, would circle the equator almost four times. To burn them in a year, you'll need to burn just over 2.7 million bills a day—enough to reach from London to Paris, and then some. How uncomfortable did that feel?

Each year, many of the world's largest companies are burning billions of dollars through the ways they manage their projects. It's popular nowadays to talk about reducing waste. But the biggest bonfire of burning billions comes from the missed opportunities in the marketplace.

Every Global 100 company creates products for its customers; each builds buildings, changes equipment, and structures deals. Support departments such as Information Technology, Legal Affairs, and Human Resources all run major projects and the speed, predictability, and productivity with which these projects are completed has a dramatic impact on how much money a company can make.

Consider the very simple case of a large company that makes ten billion dollars a year from its new products. Suppose each product could be sped up by 10 percent (for most companies, this figure is conservative). That would mean a billion dollars more in new products, each year. To look at it another way, today that company is burning a billion dollars each year. Although many factors affect both the cost and value of products moved farther along the product pipeline, the burning billions are a reality for many large companies that make blockbuster products such as airplanes, pharmaceuticals, or computer chips.

Does this seem unrealistic to you?

In this book I'll explain why it is realistic: how many companies are burning huge amounts of money, while some have learned to put out the fires and keep their money. I'll provide practical techniques you can use in your company, some of which can also help improve your daily life. I have distilled many thousands of hours of learning and experience across more than ten years, numerous consultants, and numerous client companies of many sizes and markets. This book is a 10,000-foot view of the scores of manuals, courses, and related documents that comprise our "ProChain Project Management" solution—or PPM. This solution has elements that project organizations must understand, whatever improvement initiative they undertake and whatever software they buy.

One lesson I'll stress over and over here is that tools alone are not nearly enough. "Employing tools" does not equal "achieving results." Substantial improvements do not come simply from buying software or training people. Real improvements come from positive changes in how people work and interact: behavior change. And behavior change comes from an interrelated set of tools and processes designed and tailored to produce specific results: the methodology.

The majority of companies aren't equipped to understand this lesson. They smell the smoke, but rather than implement an integrated solution to fix the behaviors that cause the fires, they buy more fire extinguishers. It's much easier to manage the tools than the people. Many Enterprise Resource Planning, Enterprise Project Management and Product Lifecycle Management applications promise to link enterprises together, implying that benefits will come. However, while these applications may provide the infrastructure for certain kinds of improvements, in the real world they are difficult to implement and very slow to generate returns. Meanwhile, the money keeps burning.

Improvements require change; substantial improvements that last over time require substantial change. The improvements that come from PPM typically require substantial change, and people often find that prospect daunting. But there's no need to be daunted, as long as you understand a few important ideas. First, the speed of change can and should be controlled through deliberate planning and execution. If someone tells you that a flip of a switch (or the installation of some software) will produce immediate benefits, run away quickly. You need a clear plan and a clear methodology to connect their solution to your problems. Second, change doesn't have to be unpleasant. The trick is to plan and communicate the changes so that all participants see the value. Third, PPM has been successfully implemented by companies of all sizes in many industries. You can do it if you want to do it.

If you're just searching for a "quick fix" or some handy tools, if you enjoy the warmth and crackle of burning money, put this book down and step away carefully. If you live in a world where you are better off without project speed, predictability, or productivity, do not continue. However, if you want a thoughtful examination of current project management practices and an understanding of how they cause companies to leave behind billions in value, if you want to recapture that value and help solidify the future of your company, please read on. The PPM system can help your company overcome these problems and avoid burning the massive amounts of money that today are going up in smoke.

Executive Overview: Searching for Billions

It's easy to see that projects can be difficult to manage. There are plenty of public failures. Industry reports continue to offer loaves of statistics amid crumbs of hope. Software vendors and consultants are multiplying like rabbits in order to fill a real need. But it doesn't matter whether others have project management problems. The question is whether your company has problems. Even if you don't have a billion-dollar problem, you may need a billion-dollar solution.

Think about which of these statements apply to your company:

- You could be much more competitive in the market if your projects were completed more quickly.
- Your projects do not normally meet their commitments.
- Your project system seems at or near the overload point, and the workload is projected to increase.
- Quality of work life is poor and employee burnout is high.
- Management's primary mechanism to control project completions is to squeeze harder, often insisting on unrealistic project completion dates.
- No matter what improvement initiatives you take on, the problems still seem to get worse.
- There are never enough resources to finish what's expected.

The PPM methodology has addressed these problems for some of the world's largest corporations. While implementation has resulted in dramatic improvements in speed, productivity, predictability, control, and communication in many industries and in companies of all sizes, ProChain's primary focus has been on larger organizations, typically in the Fortune 200. Table 1 shows some documented results. It isn't easy to collect such results, and once they are collected most large companies are unwilling to share them. So, for example, comparable results in high-tech exist, but are not yet publicly available.

TABLE 1	Fortune 200 PPM rollouts: sample results
INDUSTRY	**RESULT**
Consumer products ($5B division)[1]	5 months schedule reductions for key projects, 100% completing on time, all projects moving faster.
Medical products ($5B division)[2]	Projects were completed on average 30 days before their commitment dates; on-time performance went from 20% to 88%.
Defense contractor[3]	Repeated successes in reducing the durations of large programs by 4 months or more.
Pharma IT organization[4]	Institutionalized methodology, on-time releases, group heralded internally as "a delivery machine."
Drug development organization[5]	"Real, measurable benefits": faster projects, reliable delivery

Before proceeding further, it's important to understand where these dramatic improvements come from. The details of achieving these significant results will be addressed later in the book.

Consider how a normal project's execution might look from a high level: a series of commitments—milestones, for example— showing when various activities took place. Figure I.1 shows such a project in a Gantt-type diagram. The horizontal dimension is time, each box representing a task or chunk of work needed to complete the project. The lines represent precedence: for a task to get started, all the tasks feeding into it needed to be completed.

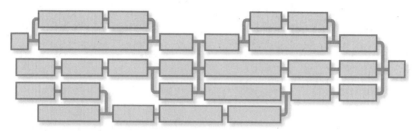

Figure I.1. Common picture

The boxes show the time frame during which the different tasks were worked, but they don't show the actual work. Very often, true milestone plans only indicate the time when task completion is required—the end of each box—rather than showing the entire time during which the task was worked. Such plans recognize that the work for each task may occur at any time before the endpoint, and that few tasks are worked without pause.

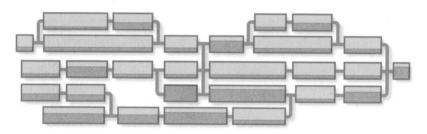

Figure I.2. Common picture (with work)

Figure I.2 shows the actual work performed during the project, represented by the height of the gold boxes. Some tasks were worked almost nonstop; some for only a small fraction of the time available. This corresponds to the reality we experience: work sits around a lot. It sits because people are simultaneously trying to work on other things; because they have phone calls, e-mails, meetings, urgent client problems; because we've lost track of the work, or of its importance. The actual fraction of time that work sits around is hard to evaluate because there may be periods where the work is intense, but the lost time can be huge. If you think this picture is unrealistic, consider how many active tasks you have right now across how many different projects. Think about the meetings, emails, and interruptions. Think about the people working on even more projects than you. The bottom line: tasks that might take days end up taking weeks. And this is the norm, not the exception.

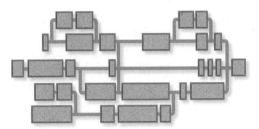

Figure I.3. Billion Dollar Picture

If we squeeze all of these tasks down to how long they might have taken, had people been working full-time on only the right things, we might get the Billion Dollar picture shown in figure I.3. In this example, assuming everyone had been able to focus on work for this project, the project *could* have been completed in about half the time.

This specific project might have gone even more quickly had we been able to identify the critical tasks. Note that the critical path—those tasks forming the longest path through the project—is much clearer in the Billion Dollar picture. Often, if we know those few places where extra effort will pay off, we *could* apply extra effort there, as additional resources or weekend work, and the project *would* be completed even more quickly.

The entire portfolio of projects could be finished more quickly if we could identify the key resources—those chronically over-loaded—and provide purposeful assistance. Despite—or perhaps because of—the chaos in which many organizations operate, the number of key resources is normally very small. Once again, to get a realistic picture of the few resources that truly need help, it's a matter of separating the wheat of figure I.3 from the chaff of figure I.1. When those resources are identified, the capabilities of the entire organization can be improved by applying capacity in a relatively small number of places.

This book is about converting an organization from the common picture to the Billion Dollar picture and beyond, a change that would be worth large bundles of money to many organizations. That conversion is conceptually very simple, because fundamentally the improved speed comes from focus: on priorities, on key tasks, on key resources. In practice, it's not simple at all. The common picture is self-reinforcing and self-fulfilling; and many of the ways people interact to sustain it are inimical to the Billion Dollar picture.

We need tools and processes that will address a number of interrelated problems:

- Uncertainty: How do you make and keep commitments in an uncertain world, without adding padding everywhere?
- Planning: How do you marshal your troops to deal most effectively with the chronic lack of resources experienced today by most organizations?
- Status: How can you tell what's really going on in a chaotic, uncertain world?
- Priorities: How do you set clear, stable priorities amid the chaos, so that people can focus on what's most important?
- Leverage: Where is it most important to focus attention, for workers, managers, and executives?
- Ownership: How can you build ownership in the kinds of changes that are needed, ownership that is a necessary component of self-sustaining change?

I'll show you—using the PPM methodology—how to answer these questions and create your own billion-dollar solution. The key to a high-impact, low-risk PPM implementation is a thorough set of principles, combined with the right tools, behavior changes, and vision, and brought to the organization through a comprehensive change management process.

Focus and Structure

People make many tradeoffs between the different basic project criteria such as time, cost, quality, and scope.[6] Given enough money, for example, delivery time can often be accelerated. Cutting scope or quality can have an impact on cost or time. With PPM, we have primarily focused on time, for a few reasons.

First, the premium associated with getting products to market more quickly is typically huge, relative to the costs, and the majority of our clients deal with new products, for which time is a huge determinant of value. "New products" includes industries such as semiconductors, pharmaceuticals, medical devices, consumer products, and aerospace. In any of these industries, the value of bringing a new product to market a day earlier can mean anywhere from thousands to millions of dollars of additional revenue. More and more companies nowadays care about how quickly and reliably their projects can complete; if you don't share these concerns, PPM is probably not for you.

Second, as we shall see, inhibitors to speed are often also inhibitors to productivity. Going faster makes people more productive and therefore less expensive. Multitasking is a pernicious evil that by itself results in substantial productivity penalties. The PPM focus on time frequently results in reduced costs and improved quality.

Third, more effective cost management can be accomplished in conjunction with a PPM implementation. When you get the control needed to gain more speed, when you have reliable and predictable project management processes, you have taken a giant step toward predicting and managing resource utilization and costs. Furthermore, you'll have the tools necessary to make informed tradeoffs between time, cost, quality, and scope.

This emphasis on speed should not be taken to mean that I believe costs are unimportant. Accounting is a critical business function; "earned value" (see Chapter 12) may be contractually required. Cost tracking tools can be effectively integrated with PPM tools. However, a detailed discussion of those tools is far beyond the scope of this book.

At the highest level, PPM is easy to describe: positive results for project organizations. But in answering the next questions— "How?" and "What does it look like for me?"—the picture gets murkier. PPM, as a methodology, includes the critical chain scheduling approach, software, and various processes. You can describe a puzzle in terms of its overall picture; you can't really describe it in terms of the individual pieces without putting them together.

Figure I.4. RACER hierarchy

A coherent description of PPM requires a strong structure. For example: suppose I told you that ability to focus on your work is good and important. Whether or not you believed me, would that stop people from interrupting you or giving you more work than you can handle?

To describe the PPM methodology—what the pieces are, how they work together, and how PPM can work for you—I rely on the building blocks shown in figure I.4.

At the top is the end result—what you're trying to achieve with PPM, the vision for the implementation. Typically the vision will have to do with project speed, predictability, and/or productivity, but discipline and quality of life might also be important.

In order to realize the vision, you'll need to activate some guiding principles; these principles are an abstract way of summarizing what you need to accomplish. Although the PPM principles seem to be common sense, concepts that everyone would agree with, they are not common practice. The heart of PPM can be found in its six guiding principles described in Part 1 of this book: the basic precepts that we are trying to make real, precepts that will get us to the vision. Principles by themselves are insufficient, but they do prepare you to understand how any company can achieve the vision of change.

Activating these guiding principles, in turn, depends on changes to behaviors (remember, the principles aren't common practice); employing the right tools to aid in changing the behaviors; and reshaping (or revising, or replacing) existing processes to use the tools and support the behaviors. Behaviors, tools, and processes are closely entwined. Certain tools imply certain behaviors, certain behaviors require certain tools, and a process is a behavior and a tool. Part 2 discusses these fundamental building blocks of the methodology. I'll repeat over and over that the tools are not the solution.[7] But good tools do help, and PPM uses many tools, including the "critical chain" scheduling approach.

With the foundation in place, we're ready, in part 3, to consider how to realize the vision. Realize the vision, activate the guiding principles, change behaviors, employ the right tools, reshape processes: implement the RACER hierarchy.

Just describing a methodology in terms of its component pieces isn't very interesting; it's like describing a ball game in terms of its rules. The components must be adapted to the playground and the players, then brought to life in actual games. That's why, throughout the book, I use the story of Imventure, a fictitious pharmaceutical company, to put the hierarchy of figure I.4 in context.

The Glossary at the end of the book defines many of the terms used in the text. You should look there first if you encounter unfamiliar terms.

Everybody's company or situation has unique characteristics, which means no examples or stories will exactly mirror your issues. You will get the most value from this book if you try to find ways that the concepts and examples presented here relate to your company, rather than looking for ways in which they are different. That will make it easier to adapt PPM to your world.

THE PPM PRINCIPLES

The starting point for understanding the Billion Dollar Solution is the center of the RACER picture, the PPM guiding principles, which form a framework for understanding the PPM approach. In this part, you'll see how these principles can be worth billions of dollars.

In order to give some ongoing context to the principles, we begin with a description of the initial situation in "Imventure."

I'll then continue with a description of the six PPM principles. Each principle is identified with a word, representing both the principle and the concepts behind it. The principle itself is laid out as a complete sentence, which is followed by a longer description. The principles are as follows:

1. Ownership
   Help everyone to understand and own the vision of the PPM implementation.

2. Leverage
   Move as quickly as possible to complete work that is highly leveraged.

3. Priorities
   Help each other to focus on the highest priorities and highest value. Strive to make them the same.

4. Status
   Communicate real status across all levels of the organization, including passing on your work when "done."

5. Planning
   Plan your work ahead of time in order to address problems when they're small.

6. Uncertainty
   Uncertainty is part of reality. Account for it explicitly and minimize its impact.

It's very important, when studying these principles, to get to the heart of the meaning. While a single word (such as "ownership") can be shorthand for the principle (in this case, "*Help everyone to understand and own the vision of the PPM implementation.*"), the principle, itself, is shorthand for a much deeper understanding: the "why" and ultimately the "how" of the principle. One goal of this book is to help you to gain that understanding, again in the context of PPM. The secret to capturing the "burning billions" and accelerating your projects lies in making these principles real.

After a discussion of the principles, Chapter 8 continues with a description of how the principles would apply in a company like Imventure.

There's an interesting irony associated with the six principles. None of the principles is particularly surprising. They are generally common sense. Therefore it's extremely common for people to be well aware that they need to follow them. They say, "We just need to have the discipline to do well those things we already know about." The problem with this philosophy is that it's very difficult to determine the combination of things that must be done together, in order to get sustainable improvements. People try to make a few changes or buy some software, and when those changes are unsuccessful they reason, "We didn't try hard enough. Let's do it again, better." And again. And again.

Some companies decide every couple of years that they need a major new initiative to improve management of projects. Often they decide to proceed with previous solutions, but to "do it better." That usually means they make no fundamental changes to how they do business, and so each time the results are the same. In his excellent book *Slack*, Tom DeMarco calls this the First Law of Bad Management: If something isn't working, do more of it.[1]

Once you have a detailed understanding of the principles, you'll be prepared for the technical aspects of the billion dollar solution, described in part 2; and the steps taken by Imventure to achieve their vision, described in part 3.

1

INTRODUCTION
TO IMVENTURE

Throughout this book the fictitious company Imventure provides a concrete example to help clarify key factors of a PPM implementation. Imventure is a Canadian pharmaceutical company that develops medications, but it could just as well be a European company that launches spacecraft or a South American company that designs blenders.[2] The specific problems presented by a given industry will vary, but most of the principles behind the solution are the same. Thus Imventure should be viewed not as a single PPM company, but as representing a combination of our knowledge and experiences across many industries and companies. You should be able to find many points of comparison between Imventure and your organization.

To understand what motivates Imventure and its people, it's important first to understand some basics about the pharmaceutical industry. Creation and testing of a new medicine can take ten to fifteen years. For each new medicine that hits the shelves, a company will typically research thousands of compounds.[3] This represents a phenomenal amount of work. While patent protection extends twenty years, by the time a drug reaches the market there may be less than five years left before other companies may legally produce generic versions. The real time a company's new product is protected may be even less because there will be competition from other drugs. New products often render older ones obsolete.

The period of time after a drug first comes on the market and before other companies may manufacture it is the period during which a company must recoup the expenses of its research and development. After that, revenues from the patented product typically go down significantly. A bigger pipeline of new medicines, across the ten- to fifteen-year span of the development process, means higher and more predictable revenues out into the future. Higher revenues means more profits to satisfy shareholder expectations, more money for research and development to pursue more treatment avenues, and more flexibility on pricing and discount programs to make drugs available to more people. Predictability means companies can make better long-term plans, which is extremely important in an industry with such a long product cycle time.

At the beginning of our story, Imventure had $6 billion (Canadian) in yearly sales. As a company, it was focused largely on post-discovery drug development, taking "promising" compounds through animal and then human testing. Clinical trials were a critical part of their business. It often partnered with other companies to develop these drugs. Imventure had a dedicated staff of thousands of personnel with a huge breadth of knowledge and experience. These people worked at Imventure to make a living, but the vast majority also worked there because they believed they were making a difference in people's lives.

Imventure's Problem

Imventure was successful and profitable. And Imventure had a huge problem.

The real blockbusters, the drugs that make hundreds of millions or even billions in sales each year, had been coming less and less frequently. The pharmaceutical industry as a whole could see its pipeline of big drugs drying up over the next five years.[4] That meant lower profits, lower stock prices, and employee layoffs.

To maintain its profitability, stock prices, and research and development organization, Imventure needed a constant pipeline of new products to sell. If they continued as they always had, Imventure leadership, along with the leadership of many other pharmaceutical companies, saw significant restructuring and lay-offs in the not-so-distant future.

To fix its problems, Imventure had two alternatives. First was to speed up development of the blockbuster products, those with the biggest potential. Every year earlier that a product could be brought to market would mean an extra year patients could benefit from the drug and an extra year Imventure could enjoy the drug's protected status. The difference might mean billions of dollars per year for high-volume drugs.

Second was to put more effort into less lucrative medicines; for example, those targeted toward more limited patient populations or conditions. Many people believe that the era of the blockbusters is over, and that drug companies will need to rely more and more on less profitable new products. A lot of "pretty good" pharmaceuticals could make up for a lack of blockbusters as long as they aren't too expensive to develop. On the other hand, sinking development resources into too many compounds that don't turn out to be profitable could turn a profitable business into a money loser.[5]

Both approaches required the same solution: improving the product development process by making it faster, more efficient, and more predictable. Imventure's leadership saw improving their product development processes—especially making them faster and more predictable—as the difference between long-term failure and success. Billions of dollars were riding on their next moves.

Imventure in Detail

The development of a medicine is a very complex process. The science is difficult and the industry is highly regulated. Many requirements, coming from both pharmaceutical companies and the various governments they deal with, must be met before a drug is deemed both efficacious and safe. The durations of some parts of the projects are actually determined by regulations and cannot be reduced.

When a drug is tested for efficacy, that efficacy is relative to specific types of use; meaning specific conditions within specific populations. The set of uses a drug is tested for is called its "indications"; these indications determine what it can be marketed for. Some tradeoffs must be made during the development process between the time and money needed to test for extra indications, versus the benefits of marketing a drug for those indications. In some ways this is analogous to extra features that might be put into a home appliance or a software application.

As is the case with many complex products, from airplanes to computer chips, drug development projects can be viewed from multiple levels. The highest-level project will include the building blocks, such as various types of clinical trials, manufacturing readiness, packaging, and marketing. Within the project for the compound, there may be lower levels of "subprojects" that contain the details of these building blocks.

A project at Imventure was managed by its Project Lead, who was responsible for making the project successful. This included making sure the overall process was on track, correct approval processes were followed, and appropriate indications were tested for. This was often a tremendous responsibility, given the millions or billions of dollars in yearly sales a drug could represent. The Project Lead therefore sometimes reported directly to senior management. A Project Lead was assisted by an Assistant Lead, who was responsible for scheduling and tracking the status of the different pieces of the project. Project Leads and Assistant Leads typically managed multiple projects at the same time.

"Project Management" at Imventure was owned by a Vice President who reported to the Vice-President of Development. Because the importance of project management was recognized at Imventure, this VP had organized a Project Management Office (PMO). The PMO was essentially a service organization, to help Project Leads manage their projects. The Assistant Leads worked for the Project Leads of the projects they were assigned to, but their functional management went through the PMO.

The Milestone Approach

Schedule milestones are specific achievements or deliverables placed at specific points in time. Very often people make distinctions between scheduled completion of individual tasks and important dates for the overall project or business. The former might be called "task due dates" and the latter "milestones." In this book I don't make a distinction between the two. They all represent intermediate commitments for different levels of the organization. Task due dates and higher-level milestones typically go hand-in-hand.

Since the overall drug development process is fairly standard, the most convenient philosophy for tracking project progress at most pharmaceutical companies is milestone-based. For example, a project that includes a clinical trial might track milestones for the regulatory qualification of different sites where a drug is to be tested, configuration and testing of tailored data entry software, completions of studies conducted by vendors, translation of materials to different languages, statistical analyses and reporting, and so on. The individual functional groups responsible for the work commit to completing the work by specific milestone dates.

Imventure used a milestone approach, supported by computerized systems that reported and tracked the milestones and associated dates. Those systems were unforgiving; even if a Project Lead said it was ok to miss a milestone date, the miss still reflected poorly on the responsible persons.

Milestones were created for more detailed tasks all the way up to the highest-level goals. High-level milestones reflected the completion of important stages in the development process, and some of their dates were reported to investors by Imventure's CEO. For example, the beginning of a set of clinical trials for a promising new drug might have been reported publicly even if the drug wasn't going to be ready for sale for two or three years. That gave investors some idea of Imventure's possible future performance. Of course, it also added more pressure to hit the milestone dates. If the CEO had to report delays on an important medicine, there would be suffering, including to Imventure's stock price.

Like many large companies, Imventure was organized in "silos." A silo is a large group within the company that performs a specific function for the organization, such as marketing, manufacturing, clinical operations or packaging. Each function had a great deal of complex and specialized expertise.

In order to see how these functional organizations were performing, they were measured in various ways. Certainly, they needed to meet their milestone dates. Regulatory wanted to make sure that Imventure complied with all the necessary regulations. Manufacturing first of all needed to make sure that quality products stayed on the market, and secondarily needed to support the manufacture of new drugs for testing. Each group had its own goals and its own milestones.

The milestone philosophy is simple: if everyone hits all their milestone dates, the company will hit all its commitments, including the ones it makes to Wall Street. This kind of predictability is the Holy Grail. Unfortunately, as with the Holy Grail, many myths have sprung up.

Schedule Give-and-Take

In their original form, milestones indicated the traveling distance to or from a particular location. They were extremely common in the Roman Empire. Schedule milestones serve a similar purpose, and are very popular in project scheduling. Schedule milestones describe a goal and tell how far away that goal is. Such milestones may or may not be associated with the activities needed to reach the goal, but the key, ubiquitous distance metric is time. When someone sees a schedule milestone he or she cares about, the one thing this individual most wants to know is the date on which it's going to be delivered.

There's a fundamental difference between traveling and scheduling milestones: traveling distances don't change. The main road from my house to the center of town is always 10.3 miles. The only way it changes is if the road itself changes. A milestone would say 10.3 miles.

Scheduling milestones, dealing with time, attempt to impose certainty on something that is inherently uncertain. Suppose, for example, instead of 10.3 miles my milestone into town said 24 minutes. That's probably an average, because if there's no traffic, it could take me 19 minutes; if there's an accident, it could take two hours. I might be kind of upset if I count on 24 minutes to travel to an important meeting and it ends up taking two hours. So if the local government that's responsible for such a marker had to express distances in terms of time, they could have a

Figure 1.1: Time milestone

serious problem: those times would never be right. The government might decide to protect itself from liability by giving estimates that err on the long side.

The same problem occurs when people have to provide scheduling milestones: too long could be ridiculous, too little could bite them if they're late. So people typically solve the problem by putting in some padding; say, enough to be 90 to 95 percent sure of finishing on time. But let's look at what happens in a real task, traveling to the center of town.

Figure 1.2 shows an idealized "probability density function" indicating the chances of my trip taking different amounts of time. The area under the curve, in some time range, indicates the probability of the trip duration being within that time range. Depending on various factors (time of day, traffic, whether I follow the speed limit, and whether a policeman stops me), I might arrive quickly. If there's some kind of accident, more factors will be in play.

Now let's change scenarios. Suppose I'm sitting at my desk working, and this distribution describes a task I do often. If I had to estimate how long the task will take, I might allow forty minutes. But someone is paying me to do this work and he expects that I'll be productive all the time. If I'm estimating forty minutes for every similar task, on average I'll be sitting around doing nothing for almost half that time. So I have to commit to doing other tasks at the same time. I have to overlap my tasks or "multitask." As we'll

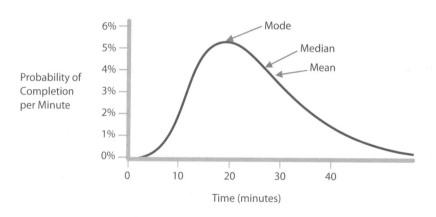

Figure 1.2: Trip to the center of town

see, multitasking is slow and inefficient. It creates chaos. And yet it was a logical, inevitable result of Imventure's milestone system. People could give aggressive times, miss their milestones a lot, and lose their jobs. Or they could give times that had, on average, padding; multitask to be sure to have enough work; and keep their jobs. They almost always chose the latter approach.

At Imventure, this give and take did result in multitasking, but—more subtly—it also blurred the lines of responsibility and accountability. A Project Lead might be responsible for getting a new product to market as quickly as possible, but the Project Lead's people were working on multiple projects and thus were not directly responsible just to the Project Lead. The Project Lead did not have full authority over them, and was often stymied in getting them to move more quickly.

Mind you, if this were all up to you or me there would be no problem. We don't much like multitasking, and we'd be perfectly happy sitting around until the next task comes along. We'd also be okay just committing to a really safe date that's further to the future. But that attitude wouldn't have gotten either of us a job at Imventure.

The counterbalance is provided by management. They may say, "Forty minutes? Are you kidding?" They may say, "You aren't working on enough tasks. Do you really want to work here?" Although I want to reduce my number of tasks and push out commitment dates, my management wants to increase the number of tasks and pull in commitment dates. This push-pull creates a huge amount of uncertainty over and above any uncertainty associated with the work itself; we'll explore this uncertainty more in Chapter 4.

The overall uncertainty also makes it difficult for management to figure out how many people to hire. If each person is working on multiple tasks, usually across multiple projects, how can you tell how many people to bring on board? You should also keep in mind that many of the people at companies like Imventure have a great deal of specialized expertise. Hiring a new person is not a matter of looking on monster.com; it can take months to find, hire, and train someone new. Also, it's considered a poor idea to hire people to meet a shortage of workers, and then find that by the time they are trained and ready the shortage has disappeared and it's time to lay them off.

As with many other companies, Imventure historically addressed the uncertainty associated with hiring through more and more outsourcing. It hired companies to provide individuals such as lab technicians, and it hired companies to conduct whole sections of their projects such as certain types of clinical trials. These vendor companies contributed their own milestones, of course. There were many positives to this: they had contractual penalties if they missed their milestone dates, their resources appeared to be unlimited (even if they weren't), and Imventure management could focus in other areas. But there were also negatives. In particular, each vendor task had its own built-in multitasking and its own padding, beyond the control of Imventure. After all, they didn't want to be late.

Imventure's Coping Mechanisms

At Imventure, when a task seemed behind schedule, the task's owner qualified to play a game called Schedule Chicken. Here's how it worked. When a number of people were contributing work to an important milestone and several were late, the first to admit it was blamed for the entire delay and appropriately disciplined. Everyone else, meaning those who didn't "chicken out" and speak up, enjoyed the benefits when the finish line moved later. This created a huge incentive for people to wait until the last minute to admit that they were late. In real companies, I've seen projects that the entire project team knew would be two years later than senior management expected. But nobody wanted to be the one to mention it to the CEO. Sometimes nobody chickens out, and management has that terrible, last-minute "awakening": the project is late.

The situation didn't necessarily improve when tasks were ahead of schedule. For example, suppose you're working on tasks for three different projects. One is well on track and looks like it'll meet its milestone date; the others seem to be at risk of being late. Where do you spend your time? Rather than complete your on-track task, chances are you'll work on the others. You won't make the on-track task late, but there's no value in finishing it early. In fact, there are two potential disadvantages. First, if you work on something that is early, you waste time you could be using on tasks that might be late. Second, if you complete it early people might wonder why you gave such a conservative milestone date. Who needs that?

The net result was that tasks at Imventure were rarely finished early.

With all the uncertainty at Imventure, coming from both the development process and the milestone process, you might expect that projects often missed their commitment dates. For example, suppose you have a simple project of ten tasks in a row, each with a 90 percent chance of being completed on time and nothing finishing early. The probability of finishing the overall set of ten tasks on time is about 35 percent (.9 to the tenth power). If you miss only one milestone date, you're late. Likewise, if you have ten tasks in parallel, the chance of every one completing within its 90 percent time is also 35 percent. The reality of due-date performance is harder to judge, because when a seismic event occurs (vendor problems, bad product data, and so on) the finish line gets moved. Imventure actually reported 30 percent on-time performance.

The "moving finish line" is not necessarily bad when used very sparingly, but it means that many sins are forgiven. It can encourage Project Leads to play an extreme form of Schedule Chicken. They commit to a "suggested" completion date, hoping that by the time it's obvious to everyone that the date is hopeless, it won't be their problem: the finish line has been moved or they're on a different job. And who could blame them? By the time anyone has enough data to "prove" that a commitment date is impossible, the date has become sacrosanct; it may be politically impossible even to mention it. The simplest coping mechanism at Imventure, given the general pressure people were under, was to work very hard. When things came down to the wire, twelve-hour days worked six days a week were not uncommon. The ubiquitous multitasking meant that no one could afford to take things easy, even if they suspected that their work wasn't crucial.

The lack of predictability across all levels of the organization meant that Imventure's senior management had a tough time making good decisions. Product X would be a good investment if it could be done by the fourth quarter of 2010 and took Y resources. Is that likely? Could they make it more likely by adding more resources? Who knew? In the end, milestones were virtually management's only lever to push for greater speed and efficiency. By autocratically applying pressure to milestones, they could hope that, at the very least, people would always work as hard as they could. But in keeping pressure on their end of the see-saw, management also ensured continuing lack of predictability.

In summary, Imventure experienced a surprising paradox: no matter how hard people worked or how much pressure management applied, project commitments always seemed long and always turned out to be unrealistic. And all this occurred despite the efforts of many good, well-intentioned people trying to do their best for the company.

To understand where Imventure's project management processes fell short and to provide a context for discussions of improvements, over the next six chapters we'll look at six basic, self-evident principles that companies like Imventure need to espouse in order to manage their projects well. Then we'll see how Imventure performed relative to these PPM principles.

Exercises

1. Washington State maintains a web page that allows you to estimate "95 percent reliable travel times" to and from various locations in the Seattle area. Go to http://www.wsdot.wa.gov/Traffic/Seattle/TravelTimes/reliability/ and check the travel times required for different routes at different times of day. If you had a critical appointment, would you trust these travel times? Why or why not?

2. Have you ever done a home improvement project? If so, compare the management of that project to the description of Imventure's management approach. What are the similarities? Do you think there may be common project management paradigms at work?

2

FIRST PRINCIPLE: OWNERSHIP

Help everyone to understand and own the vision of the PPM implementation.

If you do not know which port you sail for, there is no favorable wind.

—Lucius Annaeus Seneca

For any organizational change, it's very important to picture where you want to go, communicate that picture, and build ownership in it. That picture is your vision. If people don't see and own the vision, they will not try to achieve it and it will not happen.

A common vision for a PPM implementation includes speed and predictability. The value of speed is pretty clear: the faster you bring new products to market, the more quickly you can make money from them. Even more important (as if that's not enough), the speed gives you much more control over the market. You can capitalize on new technologies more quickly than your competitors, improve on their new strategies, and sometimes dominate new markets invented by others. This is illustrated in figure 2.1; the lighter region shows the potential benefit of speed. It is higher than

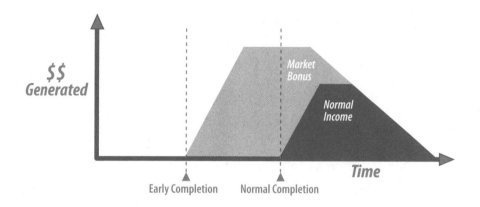

Figure 2.1. Early completion bonus

the dark area, because many times the "Market Bonus" includes the benefit of being first to gain customers.

Predictability goes hand-in-hand with speed and productivity. Predictability gives investors a sense that management is in control. Management wants predictability so as to convince one another that they're in control. In fact, it's very difficult to manage in a chaotic environment. It's like sailing a ship through a severe storm: you feel lucky to keep afloat, never mind making speed in a particular direction.

People must own the vision—for example, the need for speed, predictability, and productivity. They must feel the need themselves. Without that, the problem isn't just that you have some people not working toward this vision. The bigger problem is that you have people actively working toward other goals, which means they will resolve conflicts with your goals in a counterproductive way. Their goals are in conflict with the vision, even if no one experiences the conflicts directly. For example, research scientists are typically very interested in their research. Some have little or no interest in getting the research done more quickly to support actual products. That can mean they spend their time on various interesting technologies rather than completing research on specific, useful technologies or providing high-priority support to specific products.

People will change when they own the need for change. As long as they're waiting to see what someone else does, they're not going to change anything, and they're not going to get other people to change. Another way to put it: if people want the implementation to work, it will. Otherwise, all bets are off.

All this implies that a compelling vision statement must be something individuals in different positions can own. A vision of (for example) speed and predictability will preferably be combined with something people are likely to buy into, something that can be derived from speed and predictability. For example, the speed and predictability enabled by PPM might help enable a company to create more or better products to improve people's lives; this may be part of a vision people can own.[1]

EXAMPLE

In one PPM implementation, middle management was recognized as a problem; most of them had been around a long time and perceived no particular need to change. The manager of the implementation wanted to wait and see whether middle management would buy into the changes before strongly pushing the effort himself. That way he could minimize his personal risk if the changes weren't successful. Unfortunately, this meant he didn't try to sell a vision of the implementation. In this way he sent a message that the organization was not fully committed to the changes. The implementation only took off after the implementation manager was replaced. Even then, the "wait-and-see" message he had delivered took a long time to supplant.

To create ownership in change efforts, many companies look to tools, because tools are discrete and concrete. Enterprise Project Management (EPM) and the Project Management Body of Knowledge (PMBOK)[2] represent sets of tools that are supposed to help institutionalize "best practices." EPM is a type of software tool that typically provides the ability to share project management information across an enterprise. PMBOK is a set of standard project management practices. The problem is, if people don't understand and own the vision for the change, if they are not accountable for measurable improvements, these kinds of tools will inevitably end up helping only to solidify the status quo. If projects are managed by specific achievements or "milestones," an EPM system will help to track and manage milestones. If people do a great deal of multitasking, the EPM system will allow them to track and manage that multitasking better. Change does not come from the tools; it comes from ownership of both the need and urgency to change.

Exercises

1. List the aspects of your current job that you feel the least and the most ownership over. Which set of aspects are you most interested in? Do the aspects you have no ownership over cause you problems?
2. Describe your company's vision, and evaluate your level of ownership in that vision.
3. Pick an improvement initiative that's active in your company today and describe the vision for that initiative. How much do various people care about that vision? If your answers to these questions don't seem adequate, there's room for you to dramatically improve the chances that the initiative will be successful.

3

SECOND PRINCIPLE: LEVERAGE

Move as quickly as possible to complete work that is highly leveraged.

Mind is the great lever of all things; human thought is the process by which human ends are ultimately answered.

—DANIEL WEBSTER

Levers are "force amplifiers." A lever doesn't change the total work that's done; it enables a small force to have a large effect. If you push on a boulder, you probably won't be able to move it. If you can find a leverage point and apply pressure to it with a long enough lever, you will move it easily.

In business, not all resources and not all work are equal. Applying a "force" such as resources or attention may have no impact; in a few places, the "leverage points," a force can have a huge impact. The Pareto Principle suggests that attention in about 20 percent of those leverage points would have 80 percent of the impact.[1] The reality in organizations is normally much more dramatic. Of all possible leverage points, far more than 80 percent will result in little or no benefit and far fewer than 20 percent will have a huge impact. In *Project Management in the Fast Lane*, I spoke of a "95/1" rule, in which 95 percent of the impact is gained by focusing efforts on 1 percent of the possible leverage points.[2] We will examine several types of project-related leverage points in order to understand their significance.

> **Tip**
>
> Management books don't hide the fact that applying attention in a focused manner is critical. Normally, people have much to *do*, but the list of things that must be *done now* and *improved now* to have a significant impact is usually very short. Picking the right leverage points is important; having many people focus on them can help to synchronize an organization, potentially eliminating crippling cultural and policy issues. Many problems may look as though they need fixing, but trying to fix everything, everywhere, is usually a disaster. Those working on the non-leveraged things will dilute the efforts of those few whose work is truly critical. The ultimate effect will be the opposite of what you want: little impact and little improvement.

Direct Leverage Points

A "direct" leverage point for a project organization is one that directly involves project tasks or resources. The length of time required to complete any individual project can be determined by one of two things. The first is the *critical chain*, also known in standard terminology as the resource-constrained critical path or as the *impact chain* in PPM talk. It consists of the longest chain of tasks, taking into account any existing resource limitations. This is a significant difference from the definition of the better-known *critical path*. If, for example, you have only one software developer for a given project, it would be unrealistic to plan for more than one software development task to be performed at the same time. The critical chain and impact chain are described in detail in Chapters 9 and 10.

Typically, of all the tasks needed to complete a project, only a few are on the impact chain. This means that normally a small number of tasks determines the overall duration of a project, and the most attention should be paid to those tasks; they are leverage points.

A second type of direct leverage point, the resource, can arise when a project has many parallel paths of almost the same duration, and when tasks on those parallel paths are worked by the same set of resources. For example, in a software development project many features may need to be programmed, but those features can be developed in parallel. In the development of a semiconductor chip, many parts of the chip can be worked on in parallel by people with very similar skills. In these cases, the group of workers as a whole determines the project's duration to a much greater extent than any specific set of tasks. To a certain point—allowing for training and team building issues—the more people you have, the more features you can work on at the same time.[3] The resource is a leverage point and the impact chain is not. Adding resource capacity will have a big effect on the project's overall duration; speeding up individual tasks on the impact chain will not.

These leverage points—impact chain and resources—can overlap. That is, you can have an impact chain with tasks that must be worked in sequence due to a lack of resources. Adding more resources would allow those tasks to be worked in parallel, thereby shortening the impact chain and helping the project finish earlier.

Looking beyond individual projects to organizations, available resources often determine the overall output. A very small number of specific resource areas are usually the limiting factors, and you can't (for example) finish more projects without getting more of those resources. As an example, consider the simple production line shown in figure 3.1.

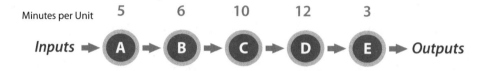

Figure 3.1. Simple production line

Suppose that each circle (A to E) represents a work cell. Raw materials (inputs) are processed starting in cell A. They move through the line from cell A to E, at which point they have been converted to products that can be sold. The time in minutes required to process the material at a given cell is shown above the corresponding circle. Supposing that each work cell can work up to forty hours per week, and assuming an unlimited market demand, what determines the output of the line?

Obviously cell D takes the most time. At twelve minutes needed per unit, it's a definite bottleneck. What's a little less obvious is that improvements for other work cells will have little or no impact. We might achieve some cost savings if, for example, we could decrease the time needed in cell C, assuming we could get rid of an employee working there. But those extra savings in one work cell are likely to be completely insignificant compared with the potential extra production for the whole line that could be gained by focusing the improvement efforts on cell D. In other words, cell D is a resource leverage point for this production line. A real production line (or project organization) may be much more complex, but it will still have very few resources that are real leverage points.[4]

The implications of organization-wide leverage points are huge. For example, if a company's ability to complete projects is limited by a very small number of resources, getting more from those resources will have a dramatic effect on the whole organization's output.[5] Most of the time, especially with larger organizations, there are many prerequisites to effectively addressing direct leverage points at the level of the organization. It isn't as simple as just hiring more people. While we'll look at techniques for addressing these organization-wide direct leverage points, this book is more focused on addressing the prerequisites, issues that must be dealt with to set up long-term success.

Indirect Leverage Points

Project organizations are very often constrained by factors less direct than resources or chains of tasks. Sometimes, for example, they are limited by people's ability to work effectively together. Therefore a critical concept in addressing any limitation is "subordination": the ability of everyone in the organization to do their best to make sure the leverage points receive the focus they need. Everyone should "subordinate" to the leverage points. In a chaotic environment, where direct leverage points are difficult to identify, there is no possibility of subordination and hence there's a great deal of wasted effort. People are not working effectively together.

Every organization is limited by its "cultural environment," which includes management style, rules, measurements (implicit or explicit), and ultimately its goal and vision. This is not inherently good or bad. Every company has limitations, and every company has a culture and a vision that shape what it can achieve. The cultural environment can be an indirect leverage point if it causes conflicts that impede a company's ability to achieve its goal or vision. This is kind of a tricky point that's worth a little discussion.

You might think that a company's cultural environment could limit the company's achievements even if it creates no conflicts, and you would be right. However, without conflicts, people will have no apparent reason to change a particular cultural element of the environment, and therefore culture is not a leverage point that you can address. It becomes more of a physical law, like gravity. For example, speed of growth is a management decision; often companies can choose to grow more quickly. However, increased growth usually implies increased risks; and responsible management of those risks imposes limits to growth. Willingness to accept risk is partly determined by culture. If a particular company is culturally very conservative, it will be unlikely to change and accept more risk unless it experiences some conflicting driver. Investor pressure to expand in order to maintain profits might create such a conflict and increase the tolerance for risk. Merely pointing out the potential for more gains will not.[6]

We frequently encounter similar cultural characteristics that could be highly leveraged. For example, some companies are planning-averse: people do not have the time or interest to plan ahead. In such cultures, planning is often viewed as a waste of time. Changing to a culture that values planning could produce tremendous gains. However, for such a culture to be a real leverage point, the lack of planning would have to cause conflicts that people want to resolve.

Some industries tend to be slower to change than others. Part of this comes from people moving from one company to another within the industry, creating accepted norms across the industry; part comes from the speed with which the industry's technology changes. For example, high-tech industries tend to jump on new ideas more quickly than most. Ability to change quickly can be a leverage point—if the lack of agility causes significant conflicts.

Exercises

1. Of all the people in your company, who are the ones doing things that, if they were able to work more quickly, would

make more money for the company? How can you tell? Check your answers with other people in your company.

2. Try to come up with three cultural elements in your company that limit its ability to achieve its vision. Do these elements create conflicts? Should they be changed? Can they realistically be changed?

THIRD PRINCIPLE: PRIORITIES

Help each other to focus on the highest priorities and highest value. Strive to make them the same.

"Begin at the beginning," the King said very gravely, "and go on till you come to the end: then stop."
—LEWIS CARROLL, *Alice in Wonderland*

If I had to pick one thing that almost all organizations or individuals could do to increase their productivity dramatically, it would be to set and maintain clear, stable priorities. Those priorities help people focus on their work; we call this focusing *Task Engagement*. The importance of focused work will become clear in the next section.

The Confetti Factory

To see why Task Engagement is so important, let's start with a simple exercise that we call the Confetti Factory. Many thousands of people have learned the importance of prioritization and focused work through this exercise since we created it in the late 1990s. It works best with several people so that you can compete for speed, but you can also close your door and try it by yourself.

Note: I strongly recommend that you actually perform this exercise; reading about it is not nearly as instructive.

Find five sheets of paper, three of one color (color A) and two of another (color B). Also get a stopwatch or some kind of timer that has a second hand.

Imagine that you are an employee of a confetti factory. This factory converts larger pieces of paper into smaller ones. As an employee, you are evaluated on your ability to work quickly and to follow orders. Each sheet of paper represents the raw material for a single task; each task is performed by converting the sheet of paper to confetti. In order to complete a task and convert a sheet into confetti, you need to make four vertical tears, creating five strips, followed by five horizontal tears on each strip. You're not allowed to overlap the paper; you must make twenty-nine tears for each sheet (see figure 4.1).[1]

To start, try a practice session with one sheet of color A, the color you have three of. Start the timer (or note the position of the second hand) and start tearing. Record your time. Count the pieces of paper you have produced; there should be thirty pieces.

Now that you've completed the training, you are a fully qualified confetti engineer. Your first challenge starts with two tasks, using one sheet of color A and one of color B. Take your two sheets and clear a work area. As your boss, I want you to produce as much high-quality confetti as possible. However, I also want you to make smooth, even progress across all your tasks so that the managers of color A and color B can both be sure that they're

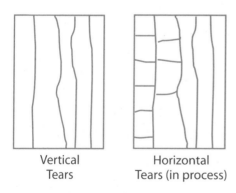

Vertical
Tears

Horizontal
Tears (in process)

Figure 4.1. Paper tears

getting equal time from you. With this in mind, after each two tears on one color, you must put that paper down and make two tears on the other color. You must switch back and forth, making even progress on each. That is the way we work in the Confetti Factory.

Start the timer and start tearing. Please do not cheat, for example by tearing several strips at the same time; that will only get you fired. But do work as quickly as possible; time is money.

Now that you have finished your first two tasks, write down your times. The times for colors A and B should be very close, only separated by one tear. Also count the number of pieces of paper of each color and write that down as well. You may not have created exactly thirty; this is a quality problem that will be counted against you shortly, when we do your performance review.

Now it's time for your second big challenge. Take your remaining two sheets of paper, clear your work area, and this time do not switch between sheets. Instead, complete one task (sheet) fully, then complete the other. In other words, no multitasking. Time the completion of tasks for color A and for color B separately. Write down your times, then count the number of pieces for each color and write those down as well.

Let's compare the results between the two challenges. The first time, because you multitasked, the work proceeded as shown in figure 4.2.

Figure 4.2. Multitasking

The second time, if you followed instructions and didn't multitask, you should have gotten something like figure 4.3:

Figure 4.3. No multitasking

There are a few peculiar things to notice when we compare multitasking with non-multitasking or "single-tasking." First, with single-tasking task A finished much earlier than it would have with multitasking. Why? Because the second time through, you just did it. You didn't go back and forth; you had clear, stable priorities and you followed them.

The second interesting point is that task B also finished earlier than it would have. That's not because you got better at tearing paper (try again if you don't believe me). It's because each switch took a little time, and when you add up all the time for all the switches it became significant. Usually we see approximately a 30 percent productivity improvement in this exercise when people single-task.

We can put the conclusions more bluntly: when there is multitasking, ***everything takes much longer***. You could have picked random priorities and stuck with them, and you would have been better off.

What about quality? Did you create thirty pieces for each task? Typically, substantially more problems arise when people are multitasking. That's because each new ball in the air makes juggling much more difficult.

Finally, consider quality of life. Which environment was more stressful? If you had to make confetti for a living, in which environment would you rather do it?

Now think about this in the context of your organization and your work. Does the Confetti Factory map to your world? How many tasks do you have on your plate? Almost without exception, people identify with the confetti factory. Senior managers and entry-level technicians alike shake their heads ruefully and say, "Yep, that's our world." Multitasking is an epidemic and it results in serious losses in speed, productivity, and quality in every project environment we have encountered. It is a huge contributor to the chaos of many working environments. I call that chaos the Multitasking Maelstrom.

Why do people multitask? We'll look at the question in more detail as we analyze Imventure. The simple answer is that they must. They must multitask because they do not have a system in place that creates and communicates clear, unambiguous priorities. They must multitask because everyone expects it; if you show no progress on a particular task, you are not considered a good worker. Furthermore, priorities in a company are cooperative; you can't "just say no." If person A is setting your priorities, you can't make your priorities stable, because person A may change his mind. And someone else always seems to be setting our priorities, sometimes not just A but also B, C, and the rest of the alphabet as well. In an interdependent organization, you can't set and maintain priorities alone.

Ironically, those people most in demand are consequently those who do the most multitasking, which often makes them the least efficient. As you might expect, some of the most effective people have found ways to enforce priorities and reduce their personal multitasking.[2]

There are a few common objections to single-tasking. For example, some people worry that single-tasking for a task called "wash clothes" would require loading the clothes into the washing machine, watching them, then removing them. Loading and removing the clothes are really separate tasks, separated by some minimum amount of time. Usually it won't make sense to watch them wash; you can do something else. Use common sense.

Some believe creativity requires multitasking because when you stop making progress on something, you should put it down for a while and do something else. That is sometimes valid, and to find out when I'd recommend the research of Mihaly Csikszentmihalyi, for example in his book *Flow*.[3] But "creativity" is often used as an excuse to avoid accountability for results. Again, use common sense. Understand the lessons of the Confetti Factory.

The Mancala Game

To broaden the discussion, we'll look at another interesting game, played on a standard "mancala" board (or a similarly laid out sheet of paper), as shown in figure 4.4:

Figure 4.4. Mancala game board

Take at least twelve markers (beads, coins, stones) and put them into the "Ideas" bucket. These are ideas you're waiting to turn into products as they go through your development process. Each month, you must put one marker from "Ideas" into "Start." Each month you are then allowed to move markers ahead by a total of six steps. That is, you have six steps you must spread among all your active markers or "projects." In a given month, for example, you could move one marker from bucket two to bucket eight, or you could move six markers from bucket eleven to "Complete." When moving a marker from the "eleven" position to "Complete," you have completed a project. Congratulations.

Play the game by dividing your six moves evenly across all active projects; in other words, by multitasking. After the first month, you'll have one marker in box six; after the second month, you'll have one in box three and one in box nine. You may make partial moves, for example, putting a marker halfway between eight and nine to represent eight and a half. Play for as many months as you can, preferably twelve.

How many projects have been completed? How many are in progress? (Note: the sum of the two should be the number of months you ran for.)

Now please consider this question: **when you begin a new project at the start of month thirteen, when will it finish?**

The chaos on the game board is such that it's virtually impossible to predict when anything will happen.[4] Admittedly, in this game we have half the resources we need: we get 6 moves each month, but have an entire new project to work on. This isn't normally realistic. On the other hand, it's extremely common for large organizations to have many active projects, in many cases far more projects than anyone is aware of. When you have too many projects active, you stir the Multitasking Maelstrom. How can you have predictability amid such turbulence?

By setting simple non-multitasked priorities for these projects, you would eliminate the Multitasking Maelstrom and achieve complete predictability. If necessary, you could even expedite a very high-priority project with minimal—or at least very predictable—impact on the others.

In addition, if your company were suddenly to eliminate the Multitasking Maelstrom, you would not only have much faster, more predictable projects, you would also have significantly happier and more productive people.

By eliminating the extra projects and starting a new project every two months, you could also eliminate the need for multitasking. There would be only one project to work on at any time. That apparent contradiction is a key lesson from this chapter. By limiting the number of projects that are active, you can increase company output and predictability. By limiting the number of tasks you work on, you can increase your personal output and predictability. To minimize multitasking, you must set clear, stable priorities. The most dramatic way to do that is to limit the amount of work in the queue. If you can't limit the queued-up work, you must learn to ignore most of it.

Before we leave the subject of priorities, we should analyze the principle that this chapter began with: *Help each other to focus on the highest priorities and highest value. Strive to make them the same.*

Ideally, we would set our priorities such that we're always working on the most valuable thing. That doesn't always happen. It can't possibly happen if those who are setting the priorities don't know what is most valuable. For example, if a technician has three tasks to work on and only one of them is on the critical path (or impact chain) of her project, she should clearly work on that one. If she doesn't know which one that is, she can't. Similarly, if many projects are active we might like to complete the most valuable ones first.

EXAMPLE

Lack of clear priorities is a common problem at all levels of management in companies of all sizes. For example, one resource group we worked with was part of a very large and successful company. The resource group's services were shared among several different business units in the organization, so they actually had multiple priority lists, each one different. Unsurprisingly, we found that the project acknowledged by senior leadership to be the most valuable in the whole company did not appear atop any of those priority lists.

Prioritization shouldn't just include tasks, but also various kinds of interruptions. Should you be constantly jumping over to email or the telephone as you do your work? Not if you want to be productive. One estimate is that 28 percent of each knowledge worker's day is lost due to interruptions.[5] Very often, when people want to really get things done, they'll hide somewhere no one can find them, come in early, or work evenings or weekends. We recognize intuitively that even though we're expected to multitask, we really can't. Our brains are not wired to focus on multiple things at once. When we attempt to switch our attention between several things, our thinking slows down dramatically.[6]

Tip

Try picking specific times during which meetings are allowed (e.g. mornings only or Tuesdays) so that people can better focus the rest of the time.

Tip

Very often, customer support is done by those most familiar with a product, meaning the best engineers or developers. This can greatly contribute to their multitasking and decrease their productivity. Find ways to free up those people, either by having others do technical support or by limiting the times during which they're on call.

Exercises

1. Very often multitasking is highly regarded. Sometimes people consciously take on multiple tasks just so that they seem more useful and are therefore less attractive as layoff targets. Go to monster.com, enter the word "multitask" under keywords, select a job category like "Project/Program Management," and press Search. How many jobs did you find? Do these companies want people who do or don't multitask? Why?

2. List your top ten tasks at work. Prioritize them. Which is the highest priority task you could be working on now (for example, reading this book)? Have you delayed that for a minute, an hour, a day, a week? Why? What impact have your delays had on the organization?

5

FOURTH PRINCIPLE:
STATUS

*Communicate real status across all
levels of the organization, including passing
on your work when "done."*

We shall never be able to remove suspicion and fear
as potential causes of war until communication is
permitted to flow, free and open, across international
boundaries.

—Harry S. Truman

I want everyone to tell me the truth, even if it costs him
his job.

—attributed to Samuel Goldwyn

Speak the truth and run.

—Yugoslav proverb

L et's start with a very simple example of status: passing on your
work when "done." First, this certainly raises the question,
"What is 'done'." It should normally be defined as "meets customer requirements," where your customer may be the person you

hand off your work to and/or the end recipient of value from the project. In many situations, people aren't sure of the requirements, and sometimes they're not even sure who their customer is. They therefore hang onto their work until it's not possible to hang onto it any more. The net effect is that work often sits around without progress being made.

Looking up to the next level, project status, the picture gets even murkier. Status is often expressed as: we're hitting our dates (or numbers or whatever) or we're not. We communicate in a binary way: one or zero, yes or no, good or bad. Unfortunately, the real world is not so clear-cut; it is full of fuzziness and probabilities. We may be, for example, 75 percent confident we'll complete something by a particular time. By pretending that status can be binary, we lose the gradations of black and white; we lose track of real status. As a result, we don't know what's going on with projects. Too often, management doesn't realize a project is going to be late until its deadline has passed.

If we want to see status across all levels of the organization, we need a context: Status of what? Communicated to whom? Why? One context is the typical matrix organization (figure 5.1). We have projects (typically product- or outcome-oriented) along one

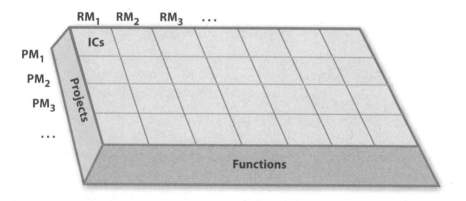

Figure 5.1. The matrix organization

dimension and functions (typically process-oriented) along the other. Resource managers (RMs, also known as functional or line managers) manage individual contributors (ICs) who do the hands-on work; project managers (PMs) manage the projects. In most large organizations this kind of structure exists, although authority and responsibility can be divided in many ways between resource and project managers. In fact, some organizations routinely oscillate between project and functionally oriented lines of authority. However the responsibilities are set up, the matrix is a reasonable way to think about an organization that has both product and process responsibilities.

One of the reasons for hierarchical organizations is to better manage the flow of status and direction. In theory, this organizational approach clarifies the lines of authority and responsibility and hence the flow of information. In practice, this is usually insufficient. People are involved in many projects and many relationships at the same time. In order to formalize "less formal" relationships, people are connected by weaker lines of authority: the "dotted line" relationships that cloud the landscape of even simple organizations. To the extent that the dotted lines muddy rather than clarify authority and responsibility, reporting becomes confused and multitasking increases.

Suppose, for example, you're programming a feature for a software module. Do you report status to your functional boss, to the project manager, or to another project manager whose work you're also doing?

Suppose you want to know whether it would be helpful to your company to delay your work and help a colleague with his task on a different project. Suppose you actually understand clearly the relative priorities of the projects because direction has been communicated from "on high." You still have to check with your project manager (perhaps through your boss) to ask whether it's ok that the feature is delayed. A valid answer requires that the project manager have a realistic picture of the importance of your task. Someone also has to check with the other project manager and find out if your colleague's task is more important than yours. It might also be useful to check whether there's someone else available whom it would be better to assign to help. All this has to be synchronized in a world where the project managers are valued for the completion of their projects and where you're being valued for the completion of your work. Why would you try to help your colleague?

People do help one another, but often this has to take place under the radar. It's not standard operating procedure. In fact, there's typically less coordination than this. Very often when people work as hard as they can to complete a task quickly, the work isn't passed on to the next person or group in line; or it is passed on, but sits around waiting because the next person isn't ready for it. People get frustrated when they put in extra effort to get something done quickly only to see it sit around. Without understanding real status in a global context, people are less likely to work harder to move key tasks along or to communicate their status. Of course, if the problem is perceived as communication, the normal management solution is more meetings.

Duck Farming

Some farmers force-feed their ducks or geese in order to cause the birds' livers to increase dramatically in size. A larger duck liver means more revenue. It's a much cheaper way to produce duck liver than to raise more ducks. Some consider this process cruel, some don't; debate continues in the media and the courts.

In the same way, many managers demand the impossible of their people and projects. They force-feed people impossible requirements, in the hopes that at the very least people will produce the most they possibly can. I call this management technique "Duck Farming." It works in direct contradiction to the concept of "real status."

EXAMPLE

". . . Stalin followed Peter the Great's logic: demand the impossible from the people in order to get the maximum possible . . . The result of Stalin's purges was a new class of managers capable of solving the task of modernization in conditions of shortages of resources, loyal to the supreme power and immaculate from the point of view of executive discipline . . ."[1]

It would appear that by demanding the impossible from his people, Stalin created excellent managers. Does that sound like what happens when people are under penalty of death if they don't do the impossible? Do pigs really fly? In reality, Stalin created a class of people who would never question even the stupidest orders, who would always report status in a way that put them in the most positive light, and who were adept at gaining authority while avoiding responsibility. Stalin was a Duck Farmer.[2]

This kind of autocratic management results in a supremely dysfunctional situation that many companies find themselves in as they manage their projects. They set impossible objectives for projects in order to make sure everyone is working as hard as possible, at the same time ensuring that people have no ownership of those objectives. Workers usually react in two ways: they sweat so much that it's obvious they're doing their best, even if it doesn't help the organization (i.e. they multitask); and they deflect blame, even if it means reporting "questionable" status. Given that, how can anyone tell what's really going on?[3]

EXAMPLE

A director once asked me, "If we shouldn't put pressure on people by setting very aggressive dates, how do we motivate them and make sure they are doing the best they can?" My answer had two parts. First, people are much more motivated by reasonable requests and meaningful work than they are by arbitrary or unreasonable goals. Second, it's the job of the functional managers to review what people work on and how motivated they are and to provide feedback on their performance. The review and rewards processes should make sure the appropriate measurements and incentives are in place.

He agreed that this makes sense, but we both knew it would take much more than logical explanations to stop the Duck Farming.

The Global Picture

Another problem with global status is the understanding of what goes into the global picture. Consider the following list:

- Status of all projects (the "portfolio")
- Status of individual projects
- Which tasks and resources are still needed to complete a project
- How long it will be until the different tasks are finished
- Which resources will be available to work which tasks

You can't have credible status for any of these without someone understanding and communicating the status of things that comprise it. Good status for one item is dependent on those below it in the list. How can you honestly say that you understand a project's status, if no one understands the status of the individual tasks required for it? Meanwhile, if you do have good status it's important to share with those in the organization who can use it.

Whether you have real status information or not, decisions must be made. People frequently get in the habit of not insisting on real status because it seems much easier and more urgent just to move ahead. For example, you can't effectively assign people or prioritize tasks when project priorities haven't been set or strong silos block communication between functions; and yet, effectively or not, assignments and priorities will happen.

Poor status communication often results in the situation shown in figure 5.2. Those at the top of the organization are responsible for the organization's vision, shareholder value, market situation, and so on. Those at the bottom, carrying out the direct physical work that gets projects done, must deal with basic physical reality, including how many people are available and how many tasks one person can juggle at the same time. With a lack of clear status available to everyone who needs it, you have a disconnect. The disparate views of reality—what we want to happen versus what actually can happen—must be reconciled.

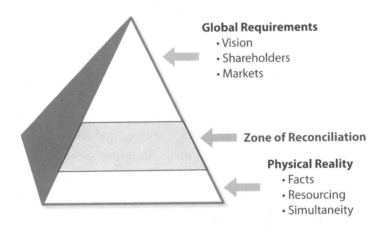

Figure 5.2. Zone of Reconciliation

It typically falls to managers in a zone in the middle of the pyramid to reconcile completion dates dictated by senior management, need for resources, project scope, and so on. This is the Zone of Reconciliation, an area of tremendous stress and churn as project and resource managers struggle to reconcile budgets and schedules between the expressed needs and physical reality.

The Zone generates a tremendous amount of spin. How many people do you need? When can this be delivered? Which projects are more important? When status passes through the Zone, the answers to many questions depend not just on the reality the organization is experiencing but on the answers people are looking for.

Many organizational cultures value accommodation over truth. The extreme case is provoked by Duck Farming, as practiced so well by Stalin. A need to accommodate creates a Zone of Reconciliation in which good decisions are difficult to make and personal success can be achieved only at the expense of organizational success. That in turn reinforces the Duck Farming mentality. In such an organization, any new system aimed at getting better status will be subverted until the needed culture changes are identified and addressed.

You might think that the Zone and its attendant poor status would drive organizational change. In reality, once accommodation has become part of the culture, it becomes invisible until it creates conflicts. Even when clear conflicts exist—for example, when projects are consistently late and over budget—people are tempted to put their energy into more Duck Farming and more tools. They rarely seek to create a culture that communicates effectively the connections between global requirements and physical reality.

Exercises

1. Considering the contents of this chapter, think about status information that is reported to you and status you report to others. At what points is status converted from real-world fuzziness to black-and-white? Do managers practice Duck Farming? To what extent is that due to lack of real status information?

2. Ask questions to dig into status information you're getting. Why do people believe what they believe? How confident are they in the status they present, and where does that confidence

come from? When there are ineffective processes, you'll often find that people's confidence comes only from other people. "Mary is a great project manager, so I believe what she tells me." That isn't bad, but it isn't enough.

6

FIFTH PRINCIPLE: PLANNING

Plan your work ahead of time in order to address problems when they're small.

Well, I'm not excusing the fact that planning and preparedness was not where it should be. We've known for twenty years about this hurricane, this possibility of this kind of hurricane.

—MICHAEL CHERTOFF,
on hurricane Katrina preparedness

The future ain't what it used to be.

—YOGI BERRA

People generally agree that planning—and specifically project planning—makes sense.[1] However, in a majority of companies people don't invest adequate resources or time in project planning, and they don't really follow the plans they create. Why is that?

Two major factors are at work here. First, while planning is generally deemed important in an abstract kind of way, there's always something urgent that can be done now. Stephen Covey discusses the "Time Management" matrix, which shows the difference between importance and urgency.[2] Urgent things typically get our attention, even if they're not very important. Meanwhile, the important things, such as planning, take a back seat. In a sense, we're too busy fighting fires to invest in fire prevention. We justify our lack of planning by pointing to all of the urgent things that need to be dealt with.

Second, project plans are often either obvious or not credible. A typical planning process consists of a project manager going to various functional managers, asking what they have to do and how long it will take, and stitching those responses together somehow to create a schedule. Often, project managers create schedules that no one believes except, sometimes, the project managers themselves.

Even large, highly successful companies frequently have very undisciplined and unsophisticated approaches to creating project plans. Sometimes important projects have no plans because the project manager recognizes the futility of creating one. In such cases it doesn't help for senior leadership to mandate that "each project shall have a plan," because the result will be a plan that no one believes in and therefore that no one uses. And data that people collect but don't use are worthless.

The "No Planning" Loop

The result of this tendency not to plan is a reinforcing loop, shown in figure 6.1 with the arrows representing "if-then" causality. Starting in the lower left of the figure, people frequently have trouble finding a good way to create credible plans. That means planning isn't valued, which means people don't generally spend much time planning and they therefore get other work to fill their time. This means they no longer have a lot of time to spend planning and so even those who value planning can't spend time on it. Over time, as planning atrophies, the logical "ready-aim-fire" impulse changes to a "ready-fire" culture. The loop in this picture shows that the ready-fire culture is self-reinforcing. Once the culture has taken hold, even if people are given a good way of creating credible plans, they won't have the time or desire to plan unless there's some external force or urgency to motivate them.

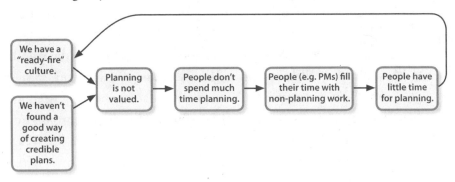

Figure 6.1. "No Planning" loop

Consider this statement: "If you follow this diet for three months, you will lose 50 pounds." The first part, "follow this diet for three months," is a prescription. "You will lose 50 pounds" is a prediction. For prescriptions to be followed, they must be credible.

Imagine that you have tried this diet for a month. If you followed the prescription and you've lost no weight, you will not believe the statement and will therefore stop following the prescription. If you've lost (say) ten pounds or more, chances are you'll continue. If you don't know whether you've lost weight or not, it will be difficult to justify continuing the diet.

Now consider this statement: "Follow this plan, and this project will finish on January 1, 2012." "Follow this plan" is a prescription, the remainder is a prediction. If you want your plan to help you address problems when they're small (i.e. a prescription that's used), it needs to be credible. To have it useful over time, it needs to be kept credible. So a good project plan, one that helps you to address problems when they're small, needs to be credible and up-to-date. It should say, "Here's what I plan on doing, here's what I expect to get from it." Without that, the plan won't be used and does not contribute to following the Planning principle.

Without good, credible planning, project teams will respond only to urgent events. They can't look ahead reliably. It's kind of like a situation in an old comic book, in which a character runs into the woods with a pot over his head. After smacking into a tree, another character asks, "Why are you running through the woods blind like that?" The response: "I missed every tree but the last one, didn't I?" Every tree we don't run into validates the lack of need for a plan. In some cases, with very experienced project teams and/or managers, their experience will help them avoid obstacles. They know the path through the forest. But heaven help them if the path changes. Commitments based on experience are better than commitments based on wishes; commitments based on experience and planning are best.

Exponential Levers

The rotational force delivered by a lever depends linearly on the length of the lever. Double a lever's length on one side of the fulcrum and you have twice the rotational force. Planning—especially project planning—is what I call an *exponential lever*. The benefits of planning are not linear relative to time; you get much more than twice the value if you go twice as far back in time to start planning. There is tremendously more value in deciding correctly whether or not to do a project than in doing it well after the commitment is made. And there is much greater value in planning how to do a project well before the major work starts, than in trying to figure out how to clean up the mess when you're partway through it.

Certain types of exponential levers are clear. For example, if you work for $15 per hour and put your money in your mattress, the increase over time is linear. But if you invest that money and get (say) 8 percent interest, the lever is exponential; interest compounds.

Project planning is not as obviously exponential. It's clear that early course corrections are simpler to make than later ones, but the main reason planning has an exponential impact is that projects build a kind of momentum over time. Various assumptions and decisions are made, vendor and distributor contracts signed, product decisions locked in. In much the same way that invested money works for you, and therefore accumulates interest exponentially, these assumptions and decisions build momentum in a particular direction. For better and for worse they inhibit your ability to change. Barry Boehm notes that reworking software at a later stage can cost 200 times as much as reworking it earlier in its life cycle.[3] Similar issues exist with the design of manufactured products.

Why plan? I once wrote, "The purpose of a project plan is to develop and/or communicate understanding of the project."[4] But I now believe it's much more than that. Planning sets and maintains your course, so that the momentum you build is in the right direction. Planning isn't putting a bunch of boxes into Microsoft Project, even though that may sometimes be part of it. Planning is a mental exercise of analysis, prediction, and communication that should happen constantly. Ultimately, good planning is a GPS system in a field where dead reckoning is commonplace. You can look at it as a tool that helps to convert the Zone of Reconciliation into a Zone of Facilitation.

Very often people think of project planning as something you do only at the start of a project. After that you start tracking. First plan, then track. This attitude destroys much of the value of planning. As you learn more, your expectations change and your plans should get better, meaning they are more useful in making predictions and decisions. As time goes by and work gets done, you should develop better estimates of how long tasks should take and what's most important. If you're not evaluating and refining your plans on a consistent, ongoing basis you miss much of the exponential value of the lever.

Here are some of the wins we've seen people achieve through ongoing, credible project planning involving all the major functions working on projects:

- Priorities that people will follow, both for individual projects and for the organization as a whole.
- Better coordination of resources, including people. ("Wow, you're doing that? I had no idea.")
- Detecting roadblocks while there's still time to remove them, without slowing down the project. ("The CCONS group is going to be a problem in six months. We'd better start working with them now.")
- Much better responses to unexpected changes. ("The regulations changed? What will be the impact of that? What do we need to do now in response?")
- Rational, data-driven justification for additional resources. ("If we had another engineer for February, we could shave an additional month from our delivery.")
- Better planning for additional people. ("I'm glad you told me this early, it'll take us six months to bring on board another person.")
- Vendor contracts that align with organizational needs. ("We need to give this vendor an incentive to finish early.")

Exercises

1. Think through the characteristics that make a lever exponential. Would you consider the discovery of antibiotics to be an exponential lever relative to growing the earth's population? Under what circumstances does the creation of intellectual property create exponential returns for a company?
2. Decide what information you would bring back, if you could look into the future. Many people, presented with such an

opportunity, would try to make money. For example, they might bring back winning lottery numbers. Project planning is a way of looking at those future lottery numbers. How clearly can you see the winning numbers for your projects?

3. We've seen that the more tasks you are trying to work at the same time, the worse your performance. Evaluate the extent to which multitasking might be considered a bad exponential lever in the way it saps your speed and productivity.

SIXTH PRINCIPLE:
UNCERTAINTY

Uncertainty is part of reality. Account for it
explicitly and minimize its impact.

War is the province of uncertainty: three-fourths of those things upon which action in War must be calculated, are hidden more or less in the clouds of great uncertainty. Here, then, above all a fine and penetrating mind is called for, to search out the truth by the tact of its judgment.

—CARL VON CLAUSEWITZ

By now, it should be clear that the six principles are closely interrelated. Planning, leverage, status, priorities, ownership— all of these are required to achieve speed and predictability over the long term. Uncertainty is at the very base of the hierarchy. How can you give real status or come up with credible plans without somehow dealing with the unknowns? In most situations in life, the things we don't know far outweigh the things we do know. Pretending certainty when there is none will be at best misleading, at worst disastrous. Whether we're driving across town or starting a war in a foreign country, if we're not honest about what we don't know, we'll make worse and worse assumptions and find ourselves in more and more trouble.

Uncertainty of Time

In this book, we deal primarily with uncertainty as it relates to time. There are obviously tradeoffs between different types of uncertainty; uncertainty of costs can be a big factor. Some ProChain clients must gain control over costs and schedules at the same time; some have the luxury of gaining speed and predictability first, then looking to better manage costs.

There are many classes of uncertainty with respect to time.[1] "Variability" can be measured through the range of possible durations for a particular task. The "known unknowns" include various risks that you can take into account and that may or may not happen. The "unknown unknowns" are completely unexpected. Suppose, for example, a student needs to predict how long a homework assignment will take. The assignment has associated variability; the student doesn't know exactly what is involved until she does it. There are known risks that homework in other subjects may take too long and affect this subject, or that the student will have to ask for help. Then there are those events that one might never expect; for example, the dog eating the homework.

Time Buffers

The PPM approach to uncertainty uses a concept made familiar by the insurance industry: "aggregation of protection," also known as "buffering." For example, very few people can protect themselves against the most catastrophic of health problems; they would have to have a huge amount of cash on hand. If everyone had to protect themselves fully, heart transplants would almost never be affordable. However, most people rarely experience a health catastrophe. By pooling funds (the insurance premium), people gain the comfort that even big problems can be solved.

With PPM, we pool safety time from project tasks into "buffers" (see Chapter 9) in order to minimize the extra time we need to ensure our commitment dates. A simple exercise can show the value of that.

Imagine a world in which projects are composed of tasks that take an average of two weeks. Half the time they take one week, but in rare cases they could take up to six or seven weeks. We can simulate this world with coin flips: The number of flips until you get heads gives the number of weeks a task takes. This exercise is best done with several people because then you will get more statistically interesting results.

Give an estimate that you have confidence in for such a task, an estimate that you can stand behind, because you'll be in trouble if you don't make it. A normal estimate would be three weeks (87.5 percent chance). If you want to be really sure or you have other work going on, too, your estimate might be higher. Flip your coin until it comes up heads; the number of flips is the number of weeks you took. Compare that with your estimate. Carry out the same procedure nine more times.

How many times, if any, did you miss your estimate? (If you do this in a group, have people who miss their estimates stand up and apologize to the class.)

On average, the estimates will be fifty percent or more over what is actually required for the tasks. What happens to that extra time in your world? Do people have to take on other work in order to fill that extra time? Does this happen to you in reality—that you estimate safe completion dates and as a consequence have to take on multiple tasks?

Now consider figure 7.1, which shows a project plan consisting of five tasks that must happen sequentially:

Figure 7.1. Simple five-task project

Using the task characteristics we've just discussed, calculate at what point in time you would place a milestone for each task to finish. Be sure you have put in milestone dates that you can commit to comfortably.

How long should the project's duration be, on average? How long is the duration based on all the milestones? See figure 7.2 for visual answers.

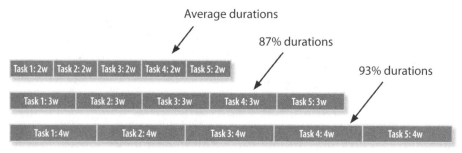

Figure 7.2. Averages vs. milestones

Which duration do you want to commit to if you're working on the project? Which duration do you want if you're responsible for all of the projects completing as early as possible?

By addressing uncertainty head-on, by looking at where uncertainty is coming from, many organizational problems can be uncovered and fixed. For example, the uncertainty of the Mancala game from figure 4.4 came *entirely* from the policies we imposed, both for starting new projects and for doing work. There is phenomenal value in uncovering these problems because they represent big opportunities to improve.

Exercises

1. Calculate how much protection you need to get an overall 87.5 percent certainty for the entire project shown in figure 7.1.[2]

2. Assuming you work in an office away from your home, estimate when you will next arrive home from work to the nearest minute. What would your estimate be if you knew you'd be fined $200 if you were wrong? What if you would lose your job? Sent to the gulag? The bigger the penalty for missing the time, the more carefully you need to protect yourself.[3]

3. Devise a survey you could give to people in your organization to assess performance relative to the PPM Principles. What do you see as the biggest obstacle to realistic results from such a survey?

4. Analyze how the presence of uncertainty affects the way companies report quarterly revenue projections and then work to those projections. What impacts does this have on the way companies actually perform?

8

IMVENTURE'S PERFORMANCE

In this chapter I'll examine the Imventure system with respect to the six PPM principles. As we go through that analysis, please continue to keep in mind that Imventure, as we've imagined it in Chapter 1, was very successful and had many smart, experienced, dedicated people. As in many real companies, those people created a system that helps billions of people and makes billions in profits each year. We may perceive inefficiencies and employees may feel that their quality of work life was not what it should be, but it's hard to argue with results. And Imventure's milestone system, with its staff of highly experienced people, had in fact achieved a profitable state of dynamic equilibrium. People generally knew what they could commit to for milestones at all levels. There were "standard times," some formal and some informal, that were generally acceptable. There was enough extra pressure that people were constantly scurrying around trying to get their work done, but usually not so much pressure that they left and went to work for the competition. Chances were, the competition was no better.

You may remember that Imventure's problem was not with the immediate picture, despite its poor on-time performance. The company was making money. The problem was that the immediate picture was changing. Imventure had to become faster, to fill up a pipeline that a few years out was looking like the Gobi Desert. It had to become more efficient, because new products would make less money. Since revenues per drug were decreasing, Imventure's management had to keep closer control over the spending of time and money, which meant they had to improve predictability. It also meant that the old silver bullet, increasing the R&D spending, was no longer appealing. Imventure needed more marketable products, not more spending. As the company attempted to push through more products as quickly as possible, its existing organization—including the people, facilities and systems—was going to be stressed.

Earlier, we examined the PPM principles in a sequence that works well in explaining their importance. If (for example) you accept the need to identify leverage points or set priorities, it becomes easy to argue that you need good status and planning. However, the reverse sequence works better in describing how the effects of the principles add together. For example, inability to deal with uncertainty, lack of planning, and lack of status are all elements that contribute to an inability to set priorities or identify and address leverage points. That's why we'll work backwards, from principle 6 to principle 1, in evaluating Imventure.

Principle 6: Uncertainty

Uncertainty is part of reality. Account for it explicitly, and minimize its impact.

Imventure ran on milestones, but their meaning wasn't always clear to those using the milestones. A milestone date could have meant a 90 percent chance of finishing on time; it could have meant "hit this date or else;" or it could have meant, "We know we'll never make it, but let's pretend for now." Given people's need to protect their completion dates, we can be very sure that milestone dates had some amount of embedded safety time during which work would be sitting around, and we can be sure that the amount of embedded time was neither obvious nor trivial. In short, Imventure dealt with uncertainty by tucking away safety time where it couldn't be managed. Management couldn't control the quantity or use of the safety time.

Ironically, despite that safety time, people's need to multitask and accept work to keep busy ensured that no matter how much safety time was present, people would have too much work to be certain of hitting their milestone dates. Switching between tasks lengthened the time needed to complete any of them, and there was inefficiency in the switching itself. Furthermore, because people were so busy there was no reason to acknowledge that project tasks often sat around, burning up time *not* being worked. This meant there was little awareness of the possibility that speed could be improved. It was a blind spot. When people did talk about going faster, they expected the cost to be borne somewhere else. "We'll make this project go faster, but we know another one will suffer."

Let's take this a step farther. The inability to quantify and deal with uncertainty meant that people at Imventure did not have the vocabulary to communicate significant elements of status. They lacked a "vocabulary of uncertainty." Yes, they might have been able to talk about probabilities, but those probabilities were at best educated guesses. An 80 or 90 percent probability of hitting a particular milestone date may mean little more than, "I'll hit it unless something happens that I haven't planned for." Meanwhile, most managers didn't want to hear a fuzzy statement like, "I might make this date." They wanted to hear, "I will make this date."

People often underestimate the importance of vocabulary. For example, imagine you're given two glasses of wine and asked, "Which wine is better?" After you give your preference, you're asked, "Why?" Chances are you won't have a good basis for answering the question. You'll have to say, "Because I like it better," which isn't very useful. Wine experts have developed a detailed vocabulary with which to discuss and compare characteristics of wines. Training in that vocabulary dramatically improves people's ability to communicate consistently and effectively about the nature and quality of wines.[1]

You can tell that people do not have a vocabulary of uncertainty when they treat uncertain events as certain. That happens very often with forecasts: "Here is the date when this will happen" or "here are our projected earnings for Q4." Sometimes people get around their lack of this vocabulary by fudging commitments. For example, management might say, "We expect this product to be on the market by Q4 of 2009." Ironically, many times you should have more confidence when people express less certainty, because they're admitting what they don't know. Such admissions can be difficult, especially for people who are supposed to have answers.

There was little interest inside Imventure in following this PPM "Uncertainty" principle. If someone spoke of uncertainty, others might hear but they didn't have the vocabulary to understand. So why bother?

Principle 5: Planning

Plan your work ahead of time in order to address problems when they're small.

Did Imventure's project plans enable people to plan their work ahead of time and address problems when they were small? Consider that Assistant Leads put together comprehensive milestone plans. They had sophisticated systems to monitor milestones and performance relative to them. People at Imventure regularly pointed to their plans and said, "We do a good job of planning." Various Assistant Leads and Project Leads also added their own techniques and processes to make the plans more effective. In fact, they had strong incentives to follow this principle, because they were responsible for the projects.

Nevertheless, Imventure's project plans showed at best spotty adherence to the Planning principle, for several reasons. First, in Imventure a milestone was a destination ("x is achieved") and a date. It didn't say what work would be needed to get to the destination. For example, a project might have had a milestone that said, "Data analysis complete." Normally, any plans that described that milestone in terms of the explicit work required, such as analysis or programming, were made within the individual functional areas and not integrated into the overall project picture.

Second, such milestones were very difficult to link to other tasks and actual resources in a meaningful way, so it was rarely done systematically for a project. Without that information, such plans had very little predictive power beyond the date itself. Without predictive power, milestone plans were primarily used to express commitments and track major delays, rather than to analyze what would happen in the future.

This was acknowledged implicitly by the Assistant Leads, most of whom used the schedules for showing status rather than for ongoing planning. They took milestone status from different resource groups and plugged it into the schedule, but unless someone missed a milestone date the updates had little impact.

And third, even if all of these problems had been dealt with, the project plans had indeterminate (but certainly large) amounts of safety built in. That made it tough to evaluate the impact of problems and respond appropriately, because people just didn't know whether the safety was sufficient to protect them. Suppose your building was built to withstand winds of 120 miles per hour and a weather forecaster said, "Hurricane Bertrand has sustained winds of 85 miles per hour with gusts of 100." That sounds pretty safe. On the other hand, if the forecaster said, "We're positive that Hurricane Bertrand has no winds of over 130 miles per hour," would you evacuate? Or would you find a new forecaster?

Principle 4: Status

Communicate real status across all levels of the organization, including passing on your work when "done."

Without good plans and without incorporating uncertainty, a company is going to have trouble scoring well on any "real status" metric. If you don't know the status, you can't communicate it. Meanwhile, the games of Schedule Chicken will always interfere.

Let's go beyond project planning and consider a range of levels of the organization. Starting at the bottom, with the most detailed work, individual task due dates have three possible statuses: on track, not on track, or complete. "On track" and "not on track" *could* be communicated, but if something is late, Schedule Chicken reduces the likelihood that it *will* be communicated. People don't want to be faulted for being late. If something is early, on the other hand, there's no particular benefit for the individual in communicating it; better to make sure that something else will also stay on track. And finally, there's little reason to communicate "complete" until the milestone date is hit. In short, you may find out the real status only when you reach the milestone date. Even that status will be suspect if people fudge the quality in order to hit the date.

At the project manager level, Inventure's 30 percent reported due-date performance made it likely that Schedule Chicken was taking place. If you're in charge of a project that's been going on for a while and looks like it's going to be late, are you going to raise the flag or play the game along with everyone else? What if you expect to be in a different job by the time people find out?

This left senior management with a difficult problem when talking publicly about products. They could report the information they had, which they knew was not accurate, or they could report an approximation. Most people preferred the latter. In the software industry, where the chance of absolute failure of a technology is far less than in pharmaceuticals, you'll still find big approximations in product announcements regarding both features and release dates.

Imventure had a problem with honest project status, but it's a tough problem for all industries. People have two reasons for exposing unpleasant truths about their own work. First, it will happen if existing processes force it, at least until people figure out how to subvert those processes. Second, it will happen if people consistently value honest status. This is the best longer-term answer, because people can learn to subvert any process. This answer can only work if everyone has confidence in the information being reported. And there is a tight connection between building trust in information quality and using the information. That trust doesn't happen over night. It's a matter of building confidence in tools, in processes, and most of all in each other: setting expectations, following through, and validating and discussing the results. This process is discussed further in Chapter 15.

Principle 3: Priorities

Help each other to focus on the highest priorities and highest value. Strive to make them the same.

It's interesting to contrast milestones and priorities. Priorities can be derived from milestones, for example by taking them in date sequence. But that's not normally done, partly because it becomes obvious that not all milestones are equally urgent or require equal work. For people at Imventure to decide what to work on, they had to judge the milestones most in danger of being missed and factor in likely new work as well as the pressure from various Project Leads.

When people at Imventure saw one project truly getting special treatment, they tended to view it in terms of the additional chaos that would occur on the other projects, those that still didn't have any priorities except "less than number one." If you gave me a rush order to put at the head of the queue, and I still had to make my other commitments, I might acknowledge the importance of speed to the company, in a vague way; but I'd certainly be upset about the effect on my work, in a very concrete way. Strict priorities were therefore viewed as win-lose arrangements. If something was number one, something else was not number one and thereby suffered. It was hard to imagine that they might move something to the front of a line of projects *without* it affecting everything else. But Imventure didn't really have a line of projects; that would imply priorities. It had a pile of projects. The irony, as we saw with the Confetti Factory, is that by setting clear priorities and converting the pile to a line, all the projects would still be better off than without priorities.

Avoiding priorities allows people to avoid decisions that may be controversial. I'd much rather avoid saying that your project is lower priority than mine; I'd rather just be friends. And priorities can be thought to give people an excuse to fail: if that's lower priority, it's ok to slack off on it. Of course, the argument is flawed; saying "Breathing is more important that eating" doesn't mean that we don't eat.

EXAMPLE

In planning a critical chain implementation for a government agency of about 100 people, we got good agreement on what we needed to achieve. We then asked what other improvement initiatives were active and got a list of about 20. Concerned that the PPM implementation could get lost among all the other initiatives, we asked the agency's director which initiative he thought was the top priority. He looked puzzled for a moment, then said, "Well . . . they all are." He didn't realize that focusing on everything means focusing on nothing.

One thing that virtually any company—Imventure included— could do to improve both speed and productivity dramatically would be to set clear, stable priorities. Unfortunately, most do not; they are mired in the milestone trap. People cannot help others to focus on the highest priorities, because there are none. Meanwhile, in many situations projects and tasks that are clearly more valuable do not get priority.

For example, a pharmaceutical company may be working on blockbuster drugs that are worth a million dollars or more for each day the product gets to market earlier, at the same time as they're working on new indications for old drugs that may be worth much less. A developer of computer printers may be working on a completely new generation of print technology at the same time as it's working on refinements to existing products. It's appropriate for a company to have a broad portfolio of products in process. While a completely new product may have a 50 percent chance of real success in the market, product refinements tend to be pretty reliable, and they help the existing product lines keep up with competitors and maintain the customer base. However, the financial advantages to getting the successful blockbuster products to market earlier are immense. Giving such products real priority, priority that keeps critical work for critical projects from sitting around idle, is difficult. Often, even when management makes the determination and flags a project as crucial, people don't know what to do with it.

Imventure didn't have good mechanisms for talking about or communicating priorities, or for making them happen. As we've seen with uncertainty, that inability to communicate about priorities leads to its own problems. While Imventure's senior management may have felt it appropriate to designate certain projects as high priority, the milestones remained milestones across the organization. There was no good way to convert them to represent priorities. That meant that even when people were told to give priority to the most important projects, they still had to hit the milestone dates on their other projects. In other words, giving a project "priority" meant saying, "This is now the most important; but everything else is still most important too."

Principle 2: Leverage

Move as quickly as possible to complete work that is highly leveraged.

Imventure did an excellent job of identifying the potential markets for its new products and calculating the probability of those products actually making it to the market. This "market awareness" is highly leveraged for a company like Imventure. That means they did have the data with which to prioritize their projects. This can be a valuable first step in making sure people work on the most leveraged things. However, the identification of a "leveraged product" rarely made the transition to real on-the-ground priorities.

Some of Imventure's Assistant Leads did create critical path plans that identified key tasks, but they had trouble getting people to give priority to those key tasks—especially if that priority might have been at the expense of something else. Part of the problem was credibility, demonstrating why other people should believe the plans. Part of the problem was in dealing with priorities, as discussed in the previous section.

Imventure had chronic resource shortages. Like every other large company, everyone was very busy (typically on many projects) and there were never enough people to go around. Management tried to balance budgets with needs. However, the chronic multitasking plus the need to protect task completion commitments ensured that no one was sure of the impact of adding or removing people.

All this meant that Imventure couldn't consistently identify the types of leverage points we discussed earlier. This made it difficult to move quickly with highly leveraged products.

Principle 1: Ownership

Help everyone to understand and own the vision of the PPM implementation.

People at Imventure owned the system as it existed. Furthermore, their system was working the way it was designed to work, and compared to the competition it wasn't working poorly.[2] However, the shared vision for the system did not include speed, predictability, or productivity.

While everyone agreed that improvements would be nice, any specific actions would likely put people in conflict with their milestone system and were therefore avoided. For example, as we've seen, it wasn't really feasible to work to priorities, and it really wasn't feasible to finish one task and then start on the next.

Like many other companies that develop new products, Imventure had been looking at Enterprise Project Management systems. They remained reluctant to jump in with both feet, investing many millions of dollars and years of people's time, because it was hard to make a direct connection between such systems and significant bottom-line benefits. However, the business pressures for action were increasing. As revenues went down, willingness to pour money into new products would go down. As more lower-value projects were attempted with minimal resources, the product development system would become more and more stressed and deliveries would become less and less reliable. Senior management recognized that a better system would be needed soon. It was not yet a life-or-death situation, but the urgency and importance were growing. Senior management was starting to own the problem, which meant that soon they would need to embrace a vision for change and create ownership in it throughout the organization.

Summary

At the start of our story, Imventure was a successful business, but problems become apparent when the company is evaluated relative to the PPM principles. There was a great deal of room for improvement. Table 2 helps express what the company did, versus what it needed in order to improve speed, predictability, and productivity. For now this table is a starting point, more of an abstract wish list than a prescriptive, exhaustive list of implementation requirements.

It's all very well to talk about principles and what people "should" do, but principles by themselves don't cause anything useful to happen. This table does hint at places where the current system has real "slop," that is, places where substantial improvements are possible that could translate directly to the bottom line. For example, just the prevalence of multitasking by itself means long wait times, which means there must be huge potential for improved efficiency and moving projects along more quickly, potential we've seen through the Confetti Factory and the Mancala Game.

Without collecting a great deal of data, it would be impossible to predict in advance just how much improvement would have been possible at Imventure by using PPM. Based on our experience in this environment, a 10 percent improvement in project speed should have been easy. Despite some approval processes that couldn't be reduced, 20 to 30 percent improvement in speed doesn't seem unreasonable, with significant productivity improvements as well. One way to improve estimates of possible results would be through a pilot project; Imventure's pilot is described in part 3. Based on data from the pilots, we can certainly imagine a billion-dollar solution for Imventure.

The biggest benefits of PPM come from continuing to perform well as the system becomes more and more stressed. You can expect that additional stresses to Imventure's system, such as more projects being worked with the same resources, would

TABLE 2	The PPM principles at Imventure		
PRINCIPLES	**MAIN IMPACT***	**IMVENTURE AT THE START**	**DESIRED**
Ownership	S, P	People owned the company vision, but across the organization there was little acknowledgment of the need for speed and no understanding of how more speed might be possible.	Everyone owns a credible vision for change that includes speed, predictability, and productivity.
Leverage	S	The market was well understood, but leverage points were difficult to identify and address.	Identify key projects, tasks and resource groups, and give them appropriate attention.
Priorities	S, P, E	Multitasking was rampant; true priorities were unclear.	Projects and tasks have clear, understood priorities that people use to minimize multitasking.
Status	S, P, E	Progress was measured against hitting or not hitting milestone dates. Because embedded protection time couldn't be seen, even key tasks sat unworked for long periods of time.	Identify key tasks and establish work rules that encourage people to work a task to "done" and then quickly pass it on.
Planning	P, E	It was difficult to talk about late milestone dates, which made it difficult to plan contingencies.	Create and use a planning and execution process that shows credible status and allows problems to be addressed while they are still small.
Uncertainty	P	There was no means of quantifying or discussing uncertainty.	Create and use a "vocabulary of uncertainty."

* S = speed, P = predictability, E = efficiency

result in extending milestone dates. That would mean adding more time to schedules, without any associated improvements in predictability. By better managing their projects, by applying PPM tools and processes, we'll see how Imventure could allow for the impact of new projects while making sure that staffing levels were appropriate.

Before diving into the next section and discussions of tools, behaviors, and processes, it's important to think briefly about the extent to which the problems we've discussed—problems that are common across many industries—are interlinked. That helps show why and how elements of the PPM solution are connected. For example, Imventure couldn't eliminate multitasking without setting priorities—at the task level and at the project level—which meant they needed to change how they dealt with milestone dates. Similarly, they couldn't gain control over uncertainty without examining the padding in individual tasks, which required changes to their planning processes.

In order to solve their problem and achieve a vision that included speed, predictability, and productivity, Imventure needed significant changes to how people worked together: the tools, behaviors, and processes they used on a daily basis. This included, among other things, building planning and reporting processes that lacked the drawbacks of their current milestone system. Despite all the changes that Imventure needed, there were many factors we could be optimistic about. They had good, experienced people and a strong, shared desire to succeed. Best of all, their need was not so urgent that they didn't have the time to plan the implementation and do it right.

In part 2, I'll describe the needed tools, behaviors, and processes before revisiting Imventure in part 3 to see how the tools look "in action."

Exercises

1. Evaluate your organization's performance relative to each PPM principle. Try taking a role-oriented view. For example, ask yourself who might feel it's in their interest to follow the principle and whether people might have reasons to follow the principle if it's not in their interest.

2. Next time you're about to board a plane, talk the airline agents into changing the boarding procedure, so that when they say, "Go!" everyone rushes to the door as quickly as possible to get on board and grab a seat. See if this is faster or more reliable than the procedure they normally use. To make it more interesting, pick a flight that's significantly over-booked.

3. You may have seen traffic lights on highway on-ramps that control the rate of cars entering the highway. List the positives and negatives of metering traffic in this way. Did you find any negatives? How do they compare with the negatives of not metering traffic?

PART

TOOLS, BEHAVIORS, AND PROCESSES

So far, I've essentially created a test—the PPM principles—that Imventure performed poorly on. It's easy to be critical and easy to set people up for failure; and in fact this is a test that the majority of companies would fail. Furthermore, it's not so easy to make the situation better. At this

point, you're probably wondering how a company like Imventure, or like your own, can change its current project management system to something that's more effective and profitable. In part 2 we'll go to the base of the pyramid of figure I.4 and examine tools, behaviors, and processes that will help to activate the guiding principles.

Tools won't solve your problems, but they can make your solutions much easier to implement. PPM has a robust tool set that will help you to reap the bottom-line returns that have been going up in smoke. In this part, we start with the *tools for an individual project*: critical chain scheduling, buffer management, and network building. These are the most fundamental tools of the PPM methodology, and they can be applied one project at a time.

You need to be able to demonstrate that you accomplished what you said you'd accomplish; without that, it's difficult for any change effort to gather and maintain momentum. So at this point we'll spend some time looking at *measurements* that ProChain has found to be helpful in assessing where an implementation is relative to where it needs to be.

Next we'll look at "*portfolio-level*" tools. The "portfolio" of projects refers to a company's set of active projects, which is in some ways very much like a portfolio of investments. Most companies have a diverse portfolio of project investments that tend to be much more interconnected than an equity investor's portfolio: resources and management are typically shared across the project investments. ProChain's capacity management and multi-project scheduling tools build on the single-project tools to help synchronize the resources, projects, and decision making.

The PPM tools can get you started dealing better with all the principles: uncertainty, planning, status, priorities, leverage, and ownership. However, some associated *behaviors* are very important to teach, such as:

- Updating projects
- Running the relay race
- Language skills
- Methodology transfer

If you want to make PPM part of the fabric of your organization, if you want to *institutionalize* it, more is needed than just tools and behaviors. Part 2 concludes with a discussion of the importance of processes, the senior-level steering team, and communication. These elements, in rigorous combination with tools and behaviors, are the main building blocks of the PPM methodology.

BASICS OF CRITICAL CHAIN SCHEDULING

Like other parts of PPM, each element of critical chain scheduling has been seen before. It is the combination of elements that allows you to change how your organization manages projects. Furthermore, scheduling by itself is of little value, compared with scheduling plus tools plus behavior change. Critical chain scheduling is only one piece of the billion-dollar puzzle.

This chapter is not intended as an in-depth discussion of the details of critical chain scheduling, but it should see you through from the perspective of understanding how PPM fits together. We'll also cover those parts of critical chain scheduling where the ProChain approach departs from the "standards."[1]

Single-Project Scheduling

The basic single-project critical chain scheduling process, the "Project Launch," is a key building block of the PPM system. It is designed to create a credible plan that can be used to enable the six principles. The scheduling process consists of several steps:

1. Create an initial project network;
2. Resolve resource contention (a.k.a. "load leveling");
3. Identify the critical chain; and

4. Create and insert protection (buffers) at strategic locations.

A project "network" is the set of tasks, task dependencies, and other information that together model the project activities. The network created in Step 1 is the starting point for critical chain scheduling. An example result of Step 1 is shown in figure 9.1 as a simple project network in a Gantt-style format. In this example, each box represents a task and the horizontal dimension is time. Finish-to-start dependences are represented by either the arrow or adjacent tasks. In each box, the task duration (in weeks) is followed by the name of the resource that does the work. Below that is the name of the task. So, for example, the leftmost task, called "Design gizmo," is expected to take two weeks and be done by the Design resource. The big diamond represents an ending milestone.

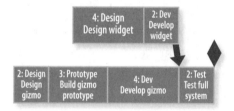

Figure 9.1. Initial project schedule

The various requirements for building an initial PPM network will be discussed in detail in Chapter 11, but here is a short summary:

- Safety time is removed from each task's duration so that it includes only estimated average "touch time," meaning the amount of hands-on time required to complete the work.
- Resources are specified. Depending on the organization and the project, these may be higher-level (e.g. a functional group

like "Engineer") or lower-level (e.g. a person like "Henrietta Applebee").

- The links between tasks are "hard" links in that they only represent dependencies we believe to be necessary.
- The task names have an active verb. They indicate the work to be done, not just the event that occurs at the end.

Next, in Step 2, we remove resource contention, also known as "load leveling." Task times are adjusted to help ensure that sufficient resources are available for all scheduled tasks at any given time. Assuming that this project has been assigned only one of each resource, figure 9.2 shows the result of step 2, load leveling:

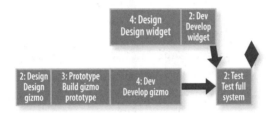

Figure 9.2. Leveled load

Resource contention has been resolved for the two tasks that use the Dev resource, assuming we have only one Dev resource available. Note that "Design widget" could be started earlier, but has been left at a late start time. In a sense, this would be a perfect schedule, if there were no uncertainty. Of course, the real world is uncertain, and we'll deal with that in the last scheduling step.

Step 3 is to identify the set of tasks that determine the project's earliest feasible completion date, known as the "critical chain." By definition, the critical chain takes into account resource dependencies. Note that in figure 9.3, the critical chain (shown in gold) hops from one Dev task to the other ("Develop gizmo" to "Develop

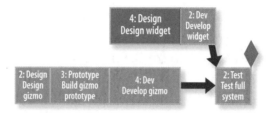

Figure 9.3. The critical chain

widget"), even though there is no hard link between these tasks. Technically we define the critical chain as the "most constrained" chain of tasks rather than the longest. For example, if "Design widget" were a vendor task and the vendor isn't starting it until 7 weeks after "Design gizmo" is started, "Design widget" could well determine the completion date of the project. In that situation, it would be on the critical chain.[2]

The critical chain is sometimes referred to in project management circles as the "resource constrained critical path," although there are differences. First, for any given endpoint we identify only one chain of tasks to be the critical chain; if a project has multiple parallel chains of the same length, we must pick just one. And second, a "critical chain" is part of a "critical chain schedule." It therefore should not be considered to exist independently of other elements of the critical chain schedule, such as buffers (described below).

The critical chain is used mainly during the scheduling process, for setting up the buffers; after that it becomes less useful. In PPM we use a different concept, the "impact chain," to help determine where to focus. There are two reasons for this. First, multiple chains of tasks may be equally critical, which, as we'll see, all fall on the impact chain; while for the critical chain we only pick one chain of tasks. And second, the critical chain only changes when you do a full reschedule, whereas the impact chain is recalculated whenever you update the status of buffers. The impact chain and buffer status indicators are described in Chapter 10.

If we've successfully removed the safety time from individual tasks, the chance of delivering this project as currently scheduled is very small. So, to improve the chance of finishing on time, the critical chain approach says we must "give back" some of the safety in the form of "buffers." Buffers are time that's needed to protect the project's delivery. The creation and insertion of buffers comprise step 4 of the critical chain scheduling process.

EXAMPLE

Start with the coin flip exercise in figure 7.1. If we protect individual tasks and attach due dates to them, the estimated duration per task would be about 3 weeks, meaning that the overall estimated duration for the project would be 15 weeks to fully protect it; while the average duration for the project should be 5 x 2 weeks = 10 weeks. But interestingly, if you allow all the tasks to start early whenever possible, you'll find that 15 weeks actually gives you a 94 percent chance of completing on time; to get 87.5 percent, you only need about 13 weeks. By pooling the safety and allowing tasks to finish and start early, we protect the overall project and save two weeks from the needed safety time.

This is the insurance principle we talked about earlier: by protecting the whole project instead of the individual tasks, we need less overall protection.

Buffers are a major part of the "vocabulary of uncertainty." They are not optional in PPM. They act as shock absorbers to protect the project, and they minimize the need for frequent rescheduling. They allow us to talk about uncertainty using concrete terms. We find two types of buffers to be most important: the project buffer and the feeding buffer.[3]

Project Buffers

Customers pay the bills, so the most important point to protect is the project completion. In order to have predictability, the customer, whether internal or external, must be protected from the uncertainty that will disrupt explicit times or milestone dates. That means we need a buffer at the end of the project, after the "Test full system" task. This buffer, called a "project buffer," is shown in figure 9.4.

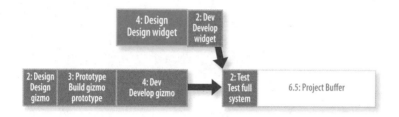

Figure 9.4. Project buffer

The entire buffer represents the range of times during which the project might be expected to complete. Despite a low probability of completing the project without consuming any buffer, there's a very high probability of completing with no more than the full buffer consumed. The project buffer end is not a milestone (note that the diamond-shaped milestone marker is missing from the picture); it's a high-probability commitment date. From the project team's perspective, you can regard the start of the project buffer as a "stretch" goal: something that would be very good to achieve, but that isn't a commitment.[4] Remember, we're changing from "hitting milestone dates," a kind of "train schedule" approach where times have to fit perfectly; to "earlier is better," a relay race.

In most projects, we can gain significant value just by removing safety time from individual tasks and putting it into a project buffer at the end. The value of managing that time explicitly and openly, rather than hiding it, is immense.

Tip

Often people fear that their customers will see buffers and respond, "What is that extra time? Get rid of it." It's possible to have an internal schedule and an external schedule, so that the customer doesn't see the buffers. That's dangerous if the customer finds out. We much prefer to enlist customer support by teaching them the language of uncertainty and buffers. In my experience, they usually appreciate that you're trying to be honest about the presence of unknowns.

Feeding Buffers

Where else is the project vulnerable? In order to better protect the project, we also "decouple" the non-critical chain tasks from the critical chain. We do that by putting a "feeding buffer" at every point where non-critical chain tasks join the critical chain. These feeding buffers help keep the critical chain tasks from sitting idle, which would cause delays. In this example, a feeding buffer would go after "Design widget." Figure 9.5 shows the result of the full four-step scheduling process.

The "Design widget" task is not scheduled at its early start. It's also not scheduled at its late start, because the feeding buffer moves it earlier. Instead, it's scheduled at the "right" start. "Design widget" is what we call a *gating task* because it has no predecessors.

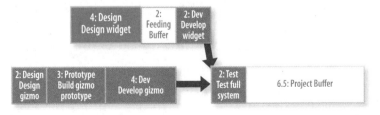

Figure 9.5. Fully buffered schedule

We don't expect it to be started as the project begins; instead, we expect it to be started three weeks after that. However, that's a decision that the project manager can override.

The next task, "Develop widget," is expected to start as soon as "Design widget" is done. It doesn't have to wait for the feeding buffer. That way, if "Develop gizmo" is ahead of schedule and frees up the Dev resource, we may also be able to finish "Develop widget" earlier, and thereby finish the project earlier.

These scheduled task times for the fully buffered schedule present a clearer picture of priorities than a schedule with tasks at their early starts. That's because the critical chain times aren't early starts or late starts; they're "when needed" starts.

Buffer Sizing

There is no definitive rule on how to set buffer sizes. In this example, we have simply taken half the length of the chain feeding the buffer. That makes the project buffer 6½ weeks long and the feeding buffer two weeks. This "50 percent rule" is the starting point that we recommend for sizing buffers.

In some cases, the 50 percent rule is overly conservative, in other cases it's aggressive. For example, if the tasks and project are very familiar to the project team—if the path through the woods is well-understood—a smaller percentage, such as 30 percent, may make sense. We've found this to be the case in some construction and routine development situations. In other cases, where there is greater uncertainty, 50 percent is insufficient.[5]

EXAMPLE

One company we worked with found, over time, that the projects for yearly releases of their standard platform product required only 10 percent project

EXAMPLE (continued)

buffers. In part this was because their task durations still had safety time in them, and in part it was because the process was very familiar to them. This didn't cause big problems until they began to develop new, less familiar products. They went from 95 percent on-time to close to zero over the course of two years until they readjusted their buffer sizing policies.

Another large company has documented 80 percent "on-time or early" project completions over a period of five years using PPM on more than 500 projects.[6] This was a huge improvement over past experience, and it was considered acceptable due to variability associated with studies and tests in their world. They define "on-time or early" to be "within three weeks of commitment." Question: should they add three weeks to their buffer sizes?

ProChain software also allows you to control the buffer contribution of individual tasks through what we call "low-risk" durations. These are estimates of how long the task might take from start to finish, if you wanted 90 percent certainty *for that task*. In the ProChain software, the default low-risk duration is twice the focused duration, and the "uncertainty" that we take a fraction of in calculating buffer sizes is the difference between the two. For example, a ten-week task would have a default low-risk duration of twenty weeks. If such a task were on the critical chain, and you used 50 percent of the difference for sizing buffers, it would contribute a net of $(20 - 10) \times 50\% = 5$ weeks to the project buffer. If the low-risk duration were instead 30 weeks, that task would contribute $7\frac{1}{2}$ weeks to the project buffer.[7]

The ability to specify a low-risk duration can be especially useful if the task truly has a fixed duration. For example, a drug study may require patient monitoring for a fixed amount of time; a vendor contract may require delivery on a specific date. These kinds of tasks should not contribute to longer buffers, assuming we believe they have little variability. In that case we would specify their low-risk durations to be the same as their focused durations.

Various other methods have been employed for sizing buffers, such as the sum-of-squares approach or Monte Carlo simulation.[8] These approaches may seem more attractive than our simple rule of thumb, because they appear more rigorous from a statistical standpoint. We've seen two practical problems with these approaches. First, they tend to result in buffers that are too small; especially for large projects. That's because the statistical approach is based on the individual tasks and their completion probabilities.[9] But individual tasks don't contain all of the information about the project or its environment. Many types of uncertainty—scope changes, key personnel leaving, major unforeseen technical risks, and so on—can't easily be modeled on a task-by-task basis, and therefore almost never are. In addition, a statistical approach provides no protection against "unknown-unknowns," the complete surprises.

The second problem with statistical approaches is that they tend to be overly complicated. Even a project team comprised of Ph.D. statisticians may not want to spend the time checking statistical assumptions in what is, after all, an uncertain environment to begin with.

We have actually tried adapting critical chain scheduling to these statistical approaches and found that the downsides—insufficient protection and greater complexity—outweigh the ephemeral upside of "statistical rigor." We have found the 50 percent rule of thumb—modified by experience and some low-risk durations—to be the simplest and best approach for most situations.

Hidden Buffers

Buffers don't have to be precise. In fact, even if all the safety is removed from tasks, even if people focus in order to work as quickly as possible, there are hidden buffers that no one wants to acknowledge publicly. Those hidden buffers are non-standard working hours—the evenings and weekends—that people often expect to have to work at the end of a project. If you truly need to hit a date and the time available for your buffer is too small, you can use the "nuclear" option and add those extra working hours to the schedule. Putting that extra time into a schedule forces people to acknowledge that the extra hours are truly happening, which forces the tradeoff to be explicit: people's spare time versus project completion. That may seem unpleasant from a management perspective, but it's actually good news, because you can figure out where the extra hours are needed—where the leverage is—and *where they're not*. Normally, only a few people really need to work long hours to finish a project as early as possible.

Tip

We've experienced several cases where a project is within six months of completion, the schedule is known to be tight, and the project team believes they will deliver on time. Everyone knows they will be working weekends and evenings for several months. A credible critical chain schedule shows that the project will inevitably be late, unless we put those extra working hours into people's calendars. Most of the time, however, people don't want to acknowledge the extra hours formally; that might even cause them to reject the critical chain schedule. That's too bad, because it can be great to know who *doesn't* have to work evenings and weekends.

Integration Risk

Some complications with feeding buffers aren't obvious from the example. Consider, for example, the project shown in figure 9.6,

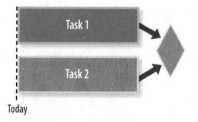

Figure 9.6. Integration risk (part 1)

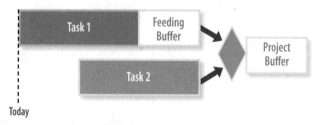

Figure 9.7. Integration risk (part 2)

where two simple tasks feed a milestone endpoint. The boxes represent tasks, without showing explicit durations or resources. The gold tasks are the critical chain.

If we add buffers to the project, we get the picture shown in figure 9.7. The feeding buffer pushes out the project. While each buffer is the correct size, the two buffers have conspired to push out the project further than we might expect. We've pushed out our commitment date to the extent that we effectively have a buffer that's 100 percent of Task 2's duration. That may seem like a lot of added protection.

Feeding buffers help protect the project against "integration risk," also known in statistics as "merge bias." When multiple tasks can be worked in parallel and then are integrated (as in figure 9.6), subsequent work can't begin until the integration occurs, which can't happen until *all* predecessors have finished. In figure 9.7, if Task 1 is early but Task 2 is late, the project won't be done until Task 2 is done, no matter how early Task 1 is. That interferes with our ability to capitalize on the early completion of Task 1. In figure

9.7, to adequately protect the project completion from this integration risk, chances are the project *does* need more protection than just a normal project buffer would provide.

> **EXAMPLE**
>
> One project team we worked with had an integration point fed by more than thirty chains, all of approximately equal length. Even though statistical demonstrations clearly showed that they were headed for trouble, they didn't want to acknowledge the need for extra time to account for integration risk. The result: they didn't allow time for integration risk, the project buffer was quickly consumed, and the project was late.

While we know that the project needs more protection due to the integration point, we don't know exactly how much. The feeding buffers are an approximate way of estimating that. In figure 9.7, the buffers may be providing too much protection; but if we had (say) ten tasks to be integrated, they could provide too little.

Because we have no perfect formula to determine "exactly" how much protection is needed because of integration points, we take several steps to refine the approximation provided by the feeding buffers. First, we make sure the network is realistic in terms of links, focused durations, and low-risk durations. Sometimes integration points can be re-thought and re-modeled to reduce their impact.

Second, we make sure that the schedule is reviewed by all key stakeholders. As a general principle, those who see the critical chain schedule must understand it. You definitely don't want a client or senior management saying, "Buffer? What buffer? Get rid of it." As an early part of that process, the project team must review the schedule and buffer sizes and try to estimate whether the buffer is too large. (Curiously, people almost never complain that the calculated buffer size is too small.) This has some dangers, because humans are not good at estimating statistics; nevertheless it's an important and necessary step. People can always override the algorithm; they must make the final decisions.

And finally, we keep in mind that it's the commitment date that the buffers are pushing out, not the actual completion date. Having a later commitment date doesn't mean that the project will be finished later. We always want people to complete tasks as quickly as possible, regardless of the buffer sizes.

Exercises

1. Suppose you have 10 tasks that must be integrated. Each task takes on average two weeks. Half of the time a task will take one week, but in rare cases it could take up to six or seven weeks. Given that an individual task has a 50/50 chance of completing in a week, what is the probability of completing the entire project in a week?[10]

2. What do you see as the major differences between the way you do scheduling today and the critical chain approach?

10

BUFFER INDICATORS

B uffer status indicators form a large part of the PPM "vocabulary of uncertainty" that is needed for people in an organization to communicate meaningfully about uncertainty and its impact. The other significant part of the vocabulary, risk management, is only dealt with peripherally in this book.

Project Buffer Indicators

Imagine now that four weeks have passed and the schedule from figure 9.5 is being updated. (This is an extreme example; we normally recommend updates at least weekly.) "Design widget" has not yet been started; "Design gizmo" has been finished, but its successor "Build gizmo prototype" has not been started. What is the status?

Figure 10.1 shows the simplest possible schedule update. The tasks haven't been moved, but today's date is indicated, and the horizontal bar through "Design gizmo" indicates that it's been finished.

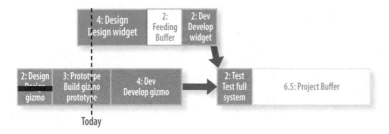

Figure 10.1. Traditional schedule update

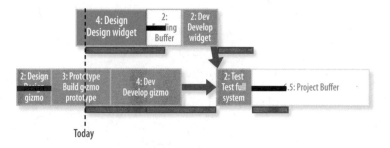

Figure 10.2. PPM update with projected times

Figure 10.2 shows the same picture, with some ProChain status indicators added. The darker bars below the tasks indicate so-called "projected times," which show the times the tasks are currently projected to be completed. The projected times for "Design widget" have pushed out by a week, which is consequently consuming a week of the feeding buffer. The critical chain tasks, on the other hand, are pushed out more. As a result, they are consuming two weeks of the project buffer.

If we look at status only as it relates to the project buffer, we get the picture in figure 10.3:

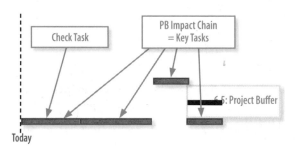

Figure 10.3. Buffer indicators

The "impact chain" for any given task in the network is the set of tasks that keeps the given task from starting earlier. The set of impact chain tasks for all the project buffers in a project (remember, a project may have multiple endpoints) is called the project's "Key Tasks." The tasks at the start of an impact chain for a buffer are referred to as the buffer's "Check Tasks," since those are the places to check immediately in order to reduce buffer consumption.

Some argue that if you're responsible for a task in a critical chain schedule, you only need dates for initial tasks of each path (the gating tasks), and then only their start dates. If it's next in priority, work it until it's done. This is technically valid, but we've found that it's very difficult to get broad buy-in without allowing people to look at projected times for their tasks. They always want some visibility into what their lives will look like.

Another useful indicator is "Percent Task Impact" or PTI, the amount—expressed in terms of buffer consumption—that a given task impacts the project buffer. The PTI of the key tasks is always equal to the project buffer consumption; if a project has multiple endpoints, it will equal the consumption of the most-consumed buffer. Other tasks (in this case, "Design widget") will have a smaller PTI. PTI is used with projected start times to set task priorities.

You can also compare project buffer consumption with "percent project completed," which is the duration of the remaining impact chain divided by the duration of the original impact chain. Looking at the critical chain, we can see that this project is 2/13 or about 15 percent complete. The project buffer is 2/6.5 or about 31 percent consumed. Buffer is being consumed more quickly than tasks are being completed, which may be a problem.

Figure 10.4 shows the percentages of buffer consumption and project completed in a Status History Chart or "fever chart." The vertical axis is percent buffer consumption, the horizontal axis is the percent project completed. The graph shows the two data points we have so far, based on the update in Figure 10.2. These two points indicate an alarming trend; indeed, if the trend continues, you can see that the project could take more than twice its originally estimated time. The good news is that fever chart analysis can be performed before you're in big trouble. In Figure 10.4, there's time to take action because there's still buffer remaining.

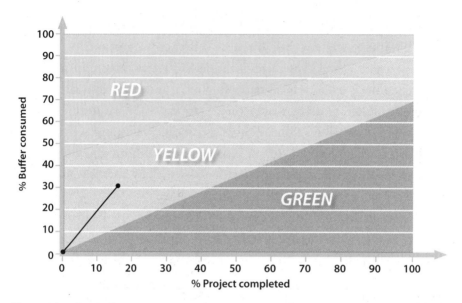

Figure 10.4. Fever chart

The regions defined by the top, middle, and bottom areas on the fever chart (typically colored red, yellow, and green respectively) indicate whether the project is in trouble. The lines slope upwards, because you don't normally need as much protection toward the end of a project as you do at the beginning. In the example, if we were down to one week of work left in the project we might believe we need a week or two of protection, but at that point the full 6.5 weeks would be excessive.

More specifically, the bottom "green" zone means the project looks likely to make its commitment date; middle or "yellow" means it is at risk; and the top "red" zone means that without intervention it looks unlikely to make its commitment date. We always expect project managers to be looking for ways to help the project go more quickly. Beyond that, specific actions depend on the project's importance and circumstances. For example, moving into the yellow zone may suggest that functional managers or their immediate superiors need to be involved; the red zone may trigger senior management intervention.

The colors are often described as watch (green), plan (yellow) and act (red).[1] This is a poor idea, since it implies management action isn't needed unless or until the project status gets into the red. For projects of significance to the organization, the project manager should always be trying to find ways to bring in the project earlier. She should seek to conserve or regain buffer.

As you use fever charts and buffers, keep in mind that small fluctuations in buffer consumption should *not* produce big reactions from management. While a couple of days delay on a mission-critical project may seem to beg for action, fluctuations are an inevitable part of normal business. A successful broker can't sell off stocks every time they experience a small loss; likewise, a successful manager must not manufacture a crisis for every fluctuation in buffer consumption.[2] However, when there are major jumps or when trends over time indicate that the existing buffer recovery plans are not working, management should absolutely intervene.

Tip

Some people like to look at "buffer burn rate," usually defined as (percent buffer remaining) / (percent longest chain of work remaining). A burn rate greater than 1 is good, smaller than 1 is bad. This is okay, but it makes me a little nervous: there's a hidden assumption that some amount of buffer consumption is all right or expected. Seek to minimize buffer consumption, not just to meet some a priori expectations.

Buffers point to places where actions can be taken to speed up projects, the "key tasks": they also add a sense of the urgency of speeding up those key tasks. In a sense, buffer reporting creates a feedback loop so that projects can't spiral too far out of control. Figure 10.5 shows the effect of that feedback: buffer recovery, as

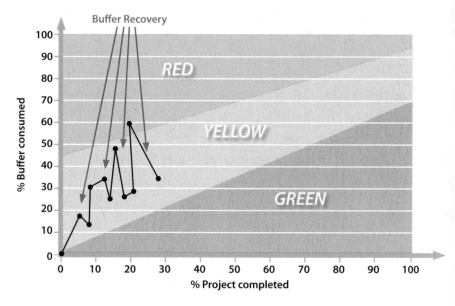

Figure 10.5. Buffer recovery (and loss)

shown by points that move sharply down and to the right. It also illustrates another phenomenon: the "out of control" work processes. Fever chart points moving significantly up and to the left indicate that work has been added to the plan; points moving down and to the right indicate successful buffer recovery. The sharpness of the fluctuations in figure 10.5 suggests potential for significant improvements to the project's planning or development processes.

Figure 10.6 shows fever chart lines for two projects. The fever chart for project A is crawling up the left side, which indicates that the project work hasn't even gotten started. Maybe it is waiting for a management approval or a vendor contract; maybe the process of getting started has identified more work. The fever chart for Project B shows no buffer consumption, which can be just as troubling. It could be a result of padded tasks in the schedules; it could be a result of people continuing to work as if their schedule is a bunch of milestones that must be met. Either case may imply a "business as usual" approach that needs to be dealt with.

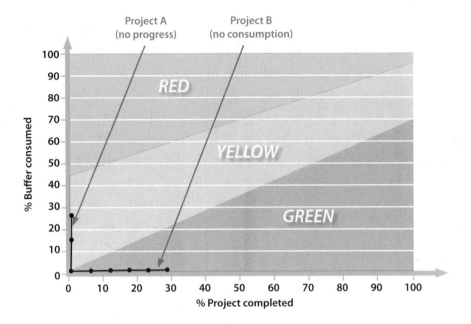

Figure 10.6. Two extreme cases

Feeding Buffer Indicators

ProChain provides the same indicators for feeding buffers as for project buffers, except that PTI and key tasks only relate to project buffers. Feeding buffer status can be tracked to make sure non-critical chains don't affect the critical chain.

We don't normally pay much attention to feeding buffer indicators, for a couple of reasons. First, feeding buffers are designed to synchronize the project schedule around the un-buffered endpoints of the original critical chain, and that situation can easily change. For example, suppose in figure 9.5 the early critical chain tasks move ahead very quickly. In terms of the overall project, the priority of the non-critical chain task "Design widget" could become high, even if it causes no feeding buffer consumption. We may not want to delay until its gating time. Similarly, if the critical chain goes more slowly than expected, even a fully consumed feeding buffer might have no real impact on the project completion. In other words, as the project continues, feeding buffer consumption often has less and less relevance to project completion.

And second, since we have indicators such as PTI that give the status of all tasks relative to the project buffers, why not use those instead? Here's another way to look at it. How hard should you have people work to avoid feeding buffer consumption? You don't know, without looking at their impact on the overall project and taking into account current project buffer consumption. So we've found it better to bypass the middle man and use PTI directly.

This de-emphasis of feeding buffers has also led us to a more intuitive approach toward integration risk. You'll note that in figure 9.7, the critical chain task is actually scheduled to start after the non-critical chain task. That doesn't make a whole lot of sense. One approach would be to start it earlier, creating a gap in the critical chain. While that may be realistic, it isn't necessarily intuitive. Furthermore, until the feeding buffer is consumed, delays won't show up in the project buffer. Instead, we usually use a software option called "Consolidate Integration Risk" that would result in the schedule shown in figure 10.7.

Everything has been moved earlier. However, because the feeding buffer (protecting us against integration risk) is consumed, we've

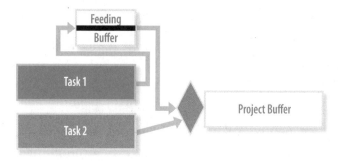

Figure 10.7. Consolidate integration risk

"consolidated" that consumed amount back into the project buffer. So the project commitment date, the end of the project buffer, is in the same place as figure 9.7, but the overall project buffer is longer. That way, rather than having a gap in the critical chain, the entire project is protected. If either Task 1 or Task 2 is late, it will show up immediately as the task dictating project buffer consumption—the "Check Task."

There is a drawback to our approach to feeding buffers: important safety time in the schedule, namely feeding buffers, is not being managed. In other words, people may use up safety and we don't know about it. By starting tasks early enough to allow for feeding buffers, and by consolidating integration risk in the project buffer, we minimize the chances of this drawback being significant.

EXAMPLE

One project manager who was resistant to the critical chain process used an interesting passive-aggressive approach. In his schedule, conceptually similar to figure 9.7, he didn't consolidate the integration risk into the project buffer. As a result, delays that consumed integration risk didn't immediately show up as project buffer consumption and therefore weren't reported to senior management. It was several months before all the integration risk (feeding buffer time) was consumed and project buffer consumption began. By then the project was already in serious jeopardy. Our preferred answer to this is to consolidate the integration risk into the project buffer, so that consumption of that safety time quickly becomes visible.

Critical Chain and the PPM Principles

Good critical chain schedules have several important characteristics that support the six PPM principles.

- **Ownership:** Well-executed PPM is a kind of relay race, and people need to own that relay-race mentality. The critical chain schedule helps, through the consensus-building process involved in its creation, by identifying critical handoffs, and by putting the focus for scheduling on speed, predictability, and productivity.

- **Leverage:** The critical chain schedule, and in particular its buffers, provides indicators that point the organization to what's most leveraged in the project. The impact chain in particular is a powerful tool that points us toward the most leveraged tasks.

- **Priorities:** A credible schedule means credible priorities. Projected times don't just give suggested task start dates; they provide a good prioritization mechanism. If you add the effect of tasks on the project buffers (the "Percent Task Impact" indicator), you have a very good mechanism to prioritize tasks within a project. Add project priorities and you have a reasonable portfolio-wide prioritization system.

- **Status:** The critical chain schedule provides real status. We've taken into account resource contention and real task links. We also have mechanisms, especially the Fever Chart, that can be used for consistent reporting of real project status across the organization.

- **Planning:** By incorporating tasks that represent real work, as well as inter-task dependencies and resources, the critical chain schedule provides a credible means of looking ahead. We can check what would happen if a small problem were to become big, and take early corrective actions.

- **Uncertainty:** Uncertainty is accounted for explicitly by removing it from tasks and putting it into buffers. This allows us to protect the schedules from the effects of uncertainty, and to manage and learn from that protection. It's difficult to overestimate the extent to which this increases the value of a schedule.

> **Tip**
>
> If your company has a Six Sigma department, check with
> them about helping implement process improvements
> identified through buffer management. PPM will help them
> to focus their efforts on what's most leveraged, and their
> Six Sigma tools will be useful as you find specific areas to
> improve.

Exercises

1. One indicator of buffer status is days of buffer remaining
   divided by days of impact chain remaining. Can this value be
   used to replace "percent buffer consumed?" How might it be
   interpreted? What are its pluses and minuses?

11

NETWORK BUILDING
OVERVIEW

Step 1 of the critical chain scheduling process, "creating an initial project network," is a critical part of the PPM system. A project network is a plan that combines resource information (such as people, functions, and calendars) and task information (such as durations, resources, and linkages between tasks) in a way that shows how we plan to fulfill the project objectives. The detailed process of pulling all this information into a project network is beyond the scope of this book. It requires, among other things, specific software (in our case, ProChain Project Scheduling and Microsoft Project) and software expertise. We include a process overview here.

Tip

If you are not familiar with critical chain network building, I strongly recommend that you find the most experienced help you can. No book can replace hands-on experience.

The PPM network building process may seem excessively involved. Some people believe that you can spend a few hours putting together a project plan and the planning process is done. That can work for simple projects with few tasks or a few people. It also works if the project plan is a pro forma exercise that people just want to be done with. However, real discipline is required to build a project plan that can be used as a basis for decision-making at all levels of the organization, over time, and the PPM process provides that discipline. With a project team that's new to PPM, with a project of one to two years involving fifty people, the process probably averages around four days of time required by a few key team members. We have found this to be, almost without exception, time well spent.

Initial Considerations

A common problem with project planning is detail. Some people want lots of detail, some want very little. Usually, 200 tasks in a single project network is a manageable number, with over 500 being very unwieldy.[1] For a reasonable-size project, we recommend starting with about 200 tasks and adding more tasks later if or when they're needed. ProChain software tools also allow for additional detail, either through subprojects (you can create multiple levels of critical chain project schedules) or through checklists (ProChain Enterprise allows you to break tasks into many pieces and assign users to them).

Be aware that when you first schedule your critical chain plan, it will probably show an end date much later than you expect. A number of factors can contribute to this, from errors in the network to unrealistic management expectations. Usually the initial project end date can be pulled in substantially, while maintaining buffers (and therefore a high probability of meeting the commitment date). It's amazing how often that process leads to innovative ideas. When those innovative ideas still don't meet business need dates, the "New Game" process described in Appendix B can still be employed.

EXAMPLE

One of my earliest experiences as a project scheduling consultant involved a pharmaceutical startup company that desperately wanted improved project predictability in order to improve credibility with its investors. It was bringing to market several cutting-edge products and had never been correct with its predictions. For eight years the CEO had been telling the market that a particular key product would be ready in two years. When the critical chain schedule was created, it said the product would be ready in about three years. The CEO was faced with a tough choice. He could tell the market that instead of taking two years, it would now be three, which would be extremely unpleasant. Or he could tell people to expunge the critical chain schedule. Which do you think he did?

Understandably, he got rid of the critical chain schedule. It was still used "underground," and proved accurate: the product was in fact released three years later.

Project promise dates can seem arbitrary to project teams when they're based solely on business needs and don't consider physical requirements. Sometimes the result of network building is a clear understanding that a project truly can't be completed when promised. One large company estimated that they could save about $1.5 million in development costs by determining reliably that a project could *not* be completed on time and therefore shouldn't be attempted.[2] For very large projects, the numbers could be much higher.

The basic network building process is shown in figure 11.1. The sections delineated by brackets to the right correspond to sections in this chapter, except that updating is dealt with in Chapter 14.

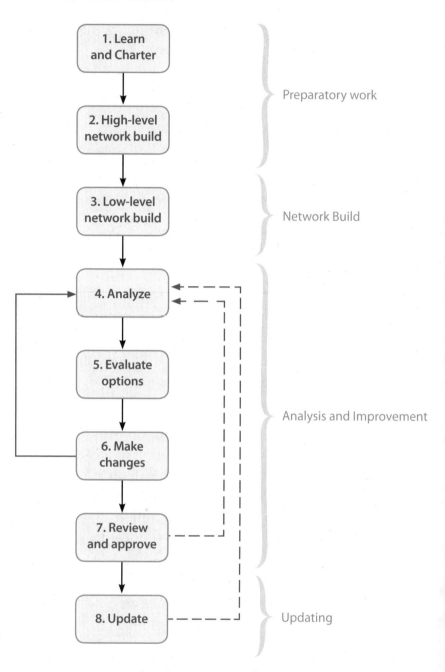

Figure 11.1. Network building process

Preparatory Work

A very important preparatory task for network building is deciding who should be on your Network Build Team (NBT). This team needs to work together to come up with a project plan that will be sufficiently credible and sufficiently comprehensive that it can be used for prioritization and decision making across all levels of the organization. The most important criterion for NBT members is organizational credibility: these should be people whose experience and vision is respected. The NBT should contain a broad range of expertise, although, sometimes, including a complete range of functions won't be possible. It should include a manageable number of people; somewhere between five and fifteen works well, with eight to ten members being ideal.

You will also need to collect concrete information describing the project, including not just technical information but also a feel for the culture. A facilitator can do this by interviewing team members. This kind of preparation pays off; even facilitators who have worked with a company for a long time can be surprised at the answers they get.

We also recommend a Project Charter document.[3] The Project Charter should include the project objectives, names and contact information for important team members, any necessary conditions for the project (such as business need dates and budgets), and major risks. We find that often even large, well-respected companies start work on projects without fully understanding these things.

To evaluate proposed ways of speeding up the project, it's also useful to make a gross measurement of the value of a day if the project were completed more quickly.

EXAMPLE

One project team found that a limiting factor on their project was some glass that took several months from order to delivery. The order for the glass couldn't be placed until they had determined the type of glass needed. Then they calculated the cost of the possible varieties of glass they might need, and discovered that they could finish the project several weeks earlier by just ordering them all. Total cost: $2,000. Total benefit: eight weeks. This was not a huge project—only a few thousand dollars a day in value—but without creating the critical chain schedule and doing the calculations, the idea of "wasting" the extra glass would not have occurred to the team.[4]

The project manager should also put together a very high-level picture of the project plan, breaking the project work into ten to twenty blocks. This normally corresponds to level two of a standard Work Breakdown Structure.[5] It should include the main phases of the project, expressed as deliverables rather than activities. Put those phases into an approximate time sequence. This high-level picture is a useful starting point for network building; you can also use it to manage the number of tasks in the network. For example, if you have eighteen high-level tasks and you want two hundred in the final project network, as a basic rule of thumb you can start by breaking each high-level task into about ten detailed tasks.

Sometimes it's not easy to decide where a "project" ends. For example, is a project complete when it's sent to manufacturing or when it's on the market actually producing revenue? To incorporate as much of the work as possible in the planning process, we prefer that endpoints be as far downstream as possible. Sometimes, because they can't visualize the detail several years into the future, people prefer to break very long, complex projects into shorter pieces. In such cases, we recommend modeling the whole project, but keeping those far-future tasks at a very high level. The detail can be added when it's feasible to do so.

At this point it's also worth giving some thought to which resources are important to model. If certain resources are typically overloaded, or if the organization has identified pacing resources (see Chapter 13), you may want to model those resources' tasks in more detail. In addition, for an organization-wide implementation, it's a good idea to plan where you're going with capacity management (also discussed in Chapter 13); that will affect the resources modeled in individual project plans.

Network Build

Project networks should have a very small number of tasks with no successors—"endpoints"—because projects usually have a small number of points where work comes together to create external deliverables. Most non-critical chain schedules that I see have many endpoints; not because the projects have many deliverables but because it's easier than figuring out what those endpoints should tie into. Furthermore, since most project management software defaults tasks to early starts, the plans look reasonable even though many linkages are missing. Given this kind of problem (among others), we find it's usually easier to scrap existing project networks and start over than to correct them.

The process for building the low-level network has two major steps. First, the team must enter and link the project tasks. We usually do that in the PERT view of Microsoft Project, projecting the view on a large screen in front of the group. Working backwards from the project objective(s) and using the high-level phases as a guide, we create and link tasks. Planning from later tasks to earlier ones helps people to look at the work from a fresh perspective, not just a backwards perspective but from the "begin with the end in mind" perspective.[6] It also helps to ensure that everything you're doing is tied to an objective.

The tasks should be only those necessary for completion of the project objectives. They should be at the level of detail we established during the preparatory work. A task should include an active verb, with notes as necessary, to help clarify the meaning. For example: "Widget XYZ" is far less descriptive than "Design and program Widget XYZ." We want the tasks to represent work needed, not milestones to be achieved.

We link the tasks as we go, making sure that the linkages represent necessary conditions. In the PPM methodology, a link doesn't say, "We expect task Y to be done after task X;" it says, "Task Y requires task X."

Once the network is constructed, we add focused durations. Ideally, these should be the "average time that should be spent on the task, assuming the resources are dedicated to that task."

In working with project teams to create a critical chain schedule, it's important to keep people thinking about why they're doing what they're doing. For example, if someone asks whether they should add a particular task, have them decide based on overall objectives: does adding the task help them to set team priorities or to meet their resource management goals? Does it add clarity or credibility? After a while, people will establish their own decision processes and make good decisions without facilitation.

Where possible and sensible, we also assign resources to the tasks. In very complex and high-level networks, the resources may be modeled more for information than leveling purposes; for detailed networks, individual functions will probably be modeled. We don't normally recommend assigning individuals to tasks, because past the next month or so it's hard to predict how the need for individuals will align across functions and projects. Depending on the project size and organization, we may at this point also associate Task Managers with tasks. A Task Manager is the person responsible for making sure one or more tasks is delivered as needed. The Task Manager could be an individual contributor, a functional manager, or a line manager.

There are many other considerations during the initial network building process. Some are illustrated in figure 11.2. This picture is derived from Figure I.2, but shows the dissection of a single task duration into its component parts.

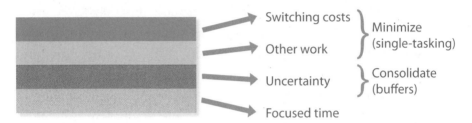

Figure 11.2. Dissecting a task duration

At the bottom is the average or "focused" time, which is what you would expect to spend on a given task on average if you were able to focus solely on it. This is the estimate you want for the PPM network. Of course, sometimes you know for a fact that you will only be able to spend a certain percentage of your time on the task. The duration can be corrected for that, but the situation should be an exception. Otherwise you are institutionalizing your multitasking.

Next is the component devoted to uncertainty, which will be aggregated into buffers. ProChain software allows you to input a low-risk or high-probability estimate, which consists of the focused duration plus the estimated uncertainty. The top two elements in the picture are normally a result of interruptions and task switching. We leave them out of the schedule because we want to minimize them.

If you think this picture looks a little like a bizarre national flag, you're right: it's the Flag of Chaos. The first step in striking these colors is to provide focused task duration estimates, estimates that are both challenging and credible. So, for example, "standard" durations would be a no-no, because they probably include a lot of extra time. Instead, try to estimate an aggressive average time. When tasks obviously have very low or very high uncertainty, we use low-risk durations to help model more accurately their contribution to buffer sizes. This helps to ensure that buffer sizes are credible.

Some people recommend taking task durations from team members, then cutting them in half, under the assumption that there will always be padding in tasks.[7] This is certainly a way to arrive quickly at challenging task durations. This is only effective when credibility, in the form of buy-in of the people working to the schedule, is not essential. That can be the case in command-and-control environments such as certain military or job shop organizations; it can also be the case for very small organizations or projects, where you can effectively persuade people to suspend their disbelief. It's not the case in the research and development or new product development worlds, where this technique will cause people to be skeptical of the resulting schedules.

When the building process is complete, we double-check the network by reviewing it from the earliest tasks to the latest. This gives a different perspective and helps to detect logic problems. We also use the ProChain software to run the first two scheduling steps (level the load and identify the critical chain). This helps provide a clearer picture of the network. If the critical chain doesn't make sense or if the leveled dates don't make sense, the team fixes the problems.[8]

Once the initial network has been created, analyzed, and improved, the full critical chain scheduling process is run, in order to see what the schedule's dates look like. At this point, it's not uncommon for the project's buffered end date to extend months or even years beyond the need date expressed by management. This is disconcerting, but normal; the team will be able to pull in the end date substantially through the analysis and improvement process.

Throughout the scheduling process, the current schedule is printed out on a plotter so that several people at once can check the network and make edits. Subject matter experts may be brought in to help with certain sections of the project that they are familiar with. There may also be pauses of a few days as team members research open issues.

Analysis and Improvement

The next part of the process is to analyze the network, in order to improve credibility, find creative ways to make the project go faster, and gain consensus between management and the project team. This is an iterative process of analyze, evaluate, revise, and (ultimately) review.

The analysis step begins by scheduling the project with the ProChain scheduling software. This creates a number of indicators that can be used to determine where to focus network reduction efforts.

Using tools like the impact chain, we ascertain which tasks and resources to focus on in order to bring in the network's endpoint(s). The following kinds of actions can be taken:

- Look at the links between tasks. Are they really necessary? Are they modeled correctly?
- Can any linked tasks be overlapped?
- Analyze task durations. Are they padded? Are there ways the work can be done more efficiently?
- Check resource utilization. Can tasks be done by other resources? Can resources be added?
- Typically vendor tasks are modeled with "must finish on" restrictions, to indicate the promised due date. Consider

whether vendor tasks and/or relationships can be changed.

- Can materials, prototypes, or other pieces be brought in from other products, projects, or vendors?
- Do minor differences to the specifications created by one group result in major differences in work done by another?

As changes are made to the network, the project plan should be rescheduled and the changes evaluated. Sometimes it takes some time to evaluate whether a change is possible; sometimes specialized expertise that's not part of the Network Building Team, such as the purchasing department, must be brought to bear.

EXAMPLE

A documentation group was on the impact chain during a schedule build. A large part of their work consisted of responding to changes tossed to them by other groups. They apparently had a choice between representing their work as a small number of very long tasks, which put them squarely on the impact chain; and breaking their work into thousands of discrete tasks, which was impractical. The scheduling process stalled, because the rest of the project team didn't believe that documentation should be on the impact chain, but the documentation people didn't believe that their work was properly represented. It turned out that, in reality, handoffs between documentation and other groups were causing them a great deal of extra work. After we worked with them on some protocols to improve their handoff processes, they were comfortable representing their work as a small number of reasonable-length high-level tasks.

Tip

Certain functions do not lend themselves well to detailed scheduling. These are typically groups that have many, many smaller tasks whose timing can't be predicted.

Documentation (often called "labeling") is one example. Site startup and enrollment for clinical trials can be this way as well. It is nearly impossible to manage each patient in a project plan; in a high-level plan, it can be difficult even to represent each site. If these kinds of functions are dictating your speed and predictability, you may need to focus on function-wide improvements, such as priorities and work rules (see Chapter 14).

ProChain also supplies mechanisms for analyzing the impact of feeding buffers on the schedule. Very often, people spend an inordinate amount of time using these tools, trying to reduce low-risk durations and the sizes of buffers. Past a certain point this becomes wasted effort, for a couple of reasons. First, the buffer sizes don't necessarily affect execution, so this doesn't really change how the work will be done, which is what produces the real benefits. And second, the buffer sizes must ultimately be measured against people's intuition. If they need to be changed, change them. You'll find out, over time, what size is appropriate for different types of projects in your organization. Generally the default 50 percent works well to start.

It is possible to classify tasks and projects, analyze task durations and project completion dates, and institute a rigorous approach to estimating task and buffer durations. Our experience is that such efforts are only useful for mature implementations, where the appropriate PPM behaviors have been established. For example, if your task durations assume some level of multitasking, duration "standards" could be misleading.

Once the analysis and improvement process reaches the point of diminishing returns, it's time to switch gears. If the buffered completion date is acceptable and the team is comfortable that the schedule is credible, the NBT reviews the schedule with the rest of the project team to validate assumptions and make sure nothing was missed. The NBT then presents the schedule to management for final approval.

In cases where the project's buffered end date doesn't meet the business need date, we have a number of options. This situation is described in the Old Game/New Game article in Appendix B.

Once the schedule is reviewed and approved by management, it is ready for day-to-day use. We'll look at that process in Chapter 14.

Exercises

1. Outline which PPM principles are violated by a planning strategy that features many project endpoints and many missing linkages.
2. Diagram your scheduling process and compare it with figure 11.1. Where are the significant differences? Why do they exist?
3. How much safety time do you think project tasks in your project plans have? Check some tasks and try to compare the bottom bar in figure 11.2 with the overall duration. What level of improvement does this imply is possible?

MEASURING SUCCESS

For any significant change initiative, including PPM, it's very important to measure what you did and how well it worked. Otherwise people will make guesses and assumptions, and base implementation decisions on poor data. How can you decide whether to roll out any improvement initiative, if you can't tell whether what you're doing is working?

You can't easily promote something as "good" if you have no validated results. After the initial promotion, a critical part of validating and reinforcing expectations that you've set comes from reporting and discussing results, as discussed in Chapter 15.[1] In this chapter we'll talk about some ways to measure implementation results and ways to describe what you've done to get them.

Shorter-Term Measurements

The ultimate test of whether projects are being completed more quickly as a result of PPM requires both the projects' finish dates and baselines to compare against. It is important to maintain project completion data, such as on-time performance and speed relative to similar projects. However, it's also important to gather data fairly quickly in order to validate that what you're doing is working. Waiting years to figure out how well an initiative is working and whether things need to be tweaked would make course corrections impossible. Unfortunately, this approach seems to be fairly common, especially with the implementations of enterprise tools.

One of the most valuable short-term results is "validated time saved." Suppose someone says, "We saved a month by talking with the vendor and focusing on this work, and it wouldn't have happened without PPM." If that's credible, if it can be validated, then it's important information.[2] In Chapter 11, we talked about the importance of evaluating the value of a day in bringing the project in earlier. If you combine that with time saved, you have an extremely powerful validation of short-term improvement. In addition, if you collect descriptions of how the time was saved, you can develop a database of best practices.

Another valuable short-term result is a survey. A survey is relatively easy to construct; in conjunction with a baseline, it can tell you a lot about what people are thinking. Figure 12.1, for example, shows a question from a ProChain survey.

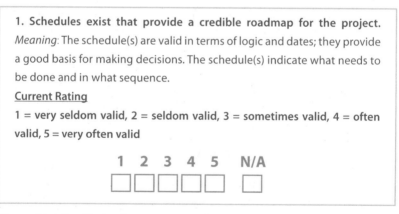

Figure 12.1. ProChain survey question

We also collect anecdotes. "This saved us a bunch of time" isn't very precise, but it certainly conveys a useful concept. The fever chart shown in figure 10.5, all by itself, shows processes that seem out of control, but are held in check by the feedback loop provided by buffer management. The value of that control mechanism is not easy to quantify, but project teams will agree that it's significant.

A less valuable short-term result is a quote. "I love this" is great to hear and it's certainly better than, "I hate this," but it doesn't translate well to company improvements. Everyone might say, "We'd love to have an extra holiday this year," but that doesn't mean it's a good idea for the company. Even if everyone loves PPM, there's no guarantee that they will actually use it to get results. It can be useful to ask managers, "In the future, if given a choice, would you manage without these tools?" If many people are saying "Yes," you may have a serious implementation problem.

You should collect these data as project networks are built and tracked, in interviews and in team meetings. Don't wait until implementation work is almost done before collecting data; by then, much of the data you want will be irretrievably lost.

Another short-term result that's even more valuable than time saved is the negatives: what's going wrong, what haven't we done, what's about to bite us. These are the things we need to fix. Without understanding and collecting the negatives, you can't fix them. Without fixing these problems, they will multiply through the course of an implementation like a virulent infection. Even problems that initially seem small can take on lives of their own. When people see problems that aren't fixed quickly, they talk about them to other people. This creates a broader impression of problems and provides ammunition to people who would prefer not to change how they work. So keep logs, manage risks, devote time in team meetings; not just to discuss what's working well but also to talk about the problems people see coming up.

Some negatives go on for so long that people stop perceiving them as problems. For example, lack of management accountability may make it very difficult to get people interested in change, strangling change efforts despite a clear need for them. Such negatives can become painfully obvious when they block progress during a

PPM implementation. They represent both severe obstacles and significant opportunities for improvement.

What We Did (and Didn't) Do

Whenever you're about to do something people may not like, including virtually any change effort, it's important first to make sure they understand what you're going to do. After you do it, you should make sure people know you did what you said you'd do. By setting expectations and then managing them, you build trust. By springing surprises, you build fear. By the same token, once you show people what they should be doing, it's important to make sure they do it.

An implementation project plan is a good mechanism to show what you plan on doing. Periodic updates and reviews help to show you did what you said you'd do. They also give you an opportunity to explain when something you expected to happen won't happen.

Another mechanism to see if people are doing what they should is the ProChain Checklist Survey, shown in figure 12.2. This exam-

Buffer Updates	**2-Jun-08**
Setup	**Status**
1. No more than one Core Team member is absent.	No
2. The Project Team Manager has calculated current buffer status.	Yes
3. The Project Manager has calculated current buffer status.	Yes
Current Status	
4. The Core Team has discussed progress on last week's key tasks and the buffer recovery plans.	Yes
5. The Project Manager has presented current buffer status to the team.	Yes

Figure 12.2. ProChain checklist survey (excerpt)

ple is a small excerpt from a monitoring tool for team meetings in which buffers are updated. Using such a tool, the team can make sure they're covering the right agenda items. Each survey question has just two states: you did it or you didn't, Yes or No. This is a great way to help protect against "confirmation bias," which is a label for people's tendency to look for things that confirm what they believe. Why not confirm objectively that teams are doing what they need to do?

You can also track checklist progress (or backsliding) over time, as shown in figure 12.3. It's a good way to ensure, over time, that a team is continuing to do the right things.

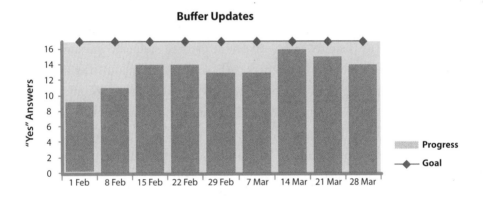

Figure 12.3. Checklist survey histogram

Longer-Term Measurements

Many types of project outcome information are routinely tracked by organizations, such as resource and budget levels, start and completion dates compared with original estimates, and level of commercial success. These data can be very useful to analyze. If you can categorize projects by types that have similar resource usage or durations, you can compare results before and after PPM.

This is helpful in both validating that the expected results are there and in justifying any ongoing need for resources to keep the implementation going.

Ongoing validation is useful in showing that expectations were met. If an implementation is not meeting expectations, that should trigger further analysis so that problems can be tracked down and solved.

It may seem that once an implementation has begun, there should be no need to justify resources, because they're already in the budget. Furthermore, longer-term measurements can take years to collect, meaning people feel little urgency to start collecting them. However, any improvement initiative that relies on dedicated personnel needs to collect data on how well it is performing. Hobbs and Aubry found that 42 percent of Program Management Offices have had their relevance or even existence seriously questioned in recent years, leading them to believe that ". . . about half of organizations are critical enough of PMOs to decide not to implement one or to seriously consider shutting theirs down if they already have one."[3] It is not unreasonable to claim that any improvement initiative needs to show ongoing value or it will be in danger of losing funding, or even being shut down.

Earned Value

"Earned value" (EV) is a measurement system that compares the budgeted costs for work scheduled within some time period ("budgeted cost for work scheduled" or BCWS), the budgeted costs for work that has been completed ("budgeted cost for work performed" or BCWP, the "earned value"), and the actual costs incurred when performing the work ("actual cost of work performed" or ACWP). The various ways of comparing and viewing these data can produce measurements of performance relative to cost, time, and scope.

EV typically has little direct place in a PPM implementation, because PPM is typically most concerned with speed, predictability, and productivity, and it deals with them well. A discussion of earned value or its integration with PPM is therefore beyond the scope of this book. However, EV is commonly used when people need to track project costs closely and it is often required for government projects. Many of our clients track earned value measurements. I have found four cautions to be important when using it, cautions that will not surprise EV experts.

- The urgency of tasks has nothing to do with the "value" that's earned. Sometimes people feel a need to maximize the "value earned," which causes them to perform work out of the preferred sequence so that the next person in line can start "earning value" as well. This is seldom the best thing for the company as a whole; schedules (preferably critical chain schedules) should be used to prioritize work.[4]
- More broadly, cost is not value. The vast majority of a project's true value is normally earned when the project has been completed. Earned value, which is normally cost-based, does not give a valid sense of what's most important to the project or the company. A key task on a project that's worth a million dollars per day is obviously much more important than a non-key task on a project that's worth a thousand dollars per day, even if they earn the same "value" according to the EV approach.
- Measurements based on deadlines impose an artificial sense of certainty. We know that tasks will sometimes take more time than originally estimated, and they should sometimes take less. Significant actions taken to hit deadlines or meet related schedule performance measures can incite destructive multitasking and game playing.

- "Percent complete" has nothing to do with time. Updating task status by collecting only percent complete results in poor estimates of how much time remains, which means you will have a poor picture of overall project status.

I have seen projects run into problems through ignorance of these cautions. Even worse, I've seen organizations interpret EV measures in ways that make game-playing inevitable, on their own projects or on their vendors' projects.

Exercises

1. Measurement is a big part of Six Sigma improvement processes. Study standard Six Sigma references in order to determine what other kinds of measurements might work for you.[5]

2. A discussion of specific measurements for different organizational roles depends a great deal on the specific organization and its human resources processes. For example, it will often be appropriate to measure project managers based on project performance, but defining that performance goes far beyond just PPM. List some of the project-related roles in your organization. Think about how the measurements described in this chapter might suggest changes to how their performance is measured.

MULTI-PROJECT MANAGEMENT

Multi-project management has many facets and a complete treatment is well beyond the scope of this book. In this chapter we'll examine the facets that are most important for PPM.

Resource Capacity Management

When we talk about capacity management, we're talking about making sure that we budget for and hire the right people at the right times to do the work that needs to be done. This is not an easy job, because hiring lead times are often long and requirements unpredictable. The following yearly steps are common in companies doing capacity management:

1. A senior-level group determines how much money is available, perhaps based on corporate dictates. It does some rough apportionment across the different resource organizations represented by the group.
2. Functional managers estimate their likely requirements for the different projects, both active and expected. They aggregate these data by quarter. Since resources are always scarce, they must try to strike a balance between what they think they'll get and what they think they need.

3. There is a set of meetings, sometimes fairly noisy and unpleasant, in which the tradeoffs between resources and projects are hashed out. Resource groups typically have too few people, marketing typically wants more products, and nobody has very good data; so some tough decisions must be made.

4. When some level of consensus has been reached, the senior person says, "Here's what it is. We're done."

Sometimes people use historical data and timesheets to estimate what will be required for future projects. It's then important to ask whether we believe the timesheets, and whether historical utilization is (or should be) a good predictor of future needs.

The Holy Grail of capacity management is the ability to match resource availability data with project resource requirements data. That allows steps 2 and 3 above to be bypassed, and step 4 to be based on real data and credible analysis. Good capacity management enhances the predictability of both budgets and project commitments. Enterprise Project Management tools are often sold based on an ability to do just this. Consider, for example, the graph shown in figure 13.1.

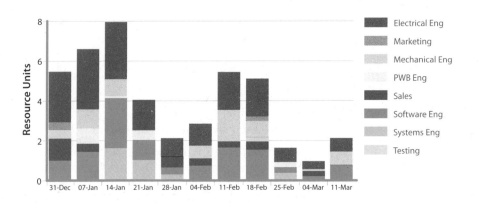

Figure 13.1. Resource load vs. time

This graph (from ProChain Enterprise) shows the units of different resources needed over time for a given set of projects. If you extrapolate this out to the future and aggregate, you can figure out budgetary requirements. Add, remove, or delay projects, and you can immediately see the impact on the resources.

Such data can be presented in many ways. Figure 13.2 shows the requirements for a particular resource (Electrical Eng), based on which tasks have the most impact on their associated project buffers. Presumably we don't want to delay high-impact tasks, and there would be less of a problem delaying medium- or low-impact tasks.

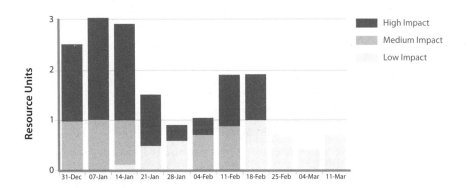

Figure 13.2. Task impacts for "Electrical Eng"

All this seems wonderful, but a number of caveats should be factored into the equation:

- The project plans on which the data are based must be credible. The PPM process is designed to create credible project plans, but this is not the norm today in most organizations. Consequently, functional managers often use very rough estimates.
- You can only look at what's modeled. The level of detail and consistency of resource modeling in project plans will be key

considerations. Non-project work, such as on-market support, meetings, and required annual training, are not normally modeled.

- People can't be 100 percent productive for extended periods of time. They have meetings and phone calls, perhaps they even need time to think.[1]

- The Multitasking Maelstrom makes it difficult to say what time is really productive and what time is not. Do you want to plan for good behavior and fix the problems that arise, or allow time for, say, rampant multitasking?

- Budgeting of resource time (and money) has variability in the same way that project time does. Therefore budgets should ideally have their own buffers. But inclusion of buffers or "management reserve" can lead to conflicts with what is considered responsible fiscal management.

In short, there's no silver bullet for capacity management. There are, however, several things you can do using PPM to make major improvements in your capacity management processes:

1. Get control over more and more individual projects. This includes creating PPM project plans, establishing clear priorities within and between projects, and reducing multitasking—at least on key tasks.

2. Plan a clear resource management strategy to use as you develop project schedules. Determine which resources you must model in detail and the resulting impact on the planning process. More detailed resource planning requires more detailed project schedules; that takes time and effort. The impact must be thought through carefully to balance costs and benefits.

3. Create a process for building and maintaining templates that can be used to estimate the approximate resource requirements for different types of projects. Templates are used for longer-

term planning, in order to account for projects that haven't yet been scheduled or fully defined. They may also be useful as starting points for creating operational PPM schedules.

4. Estimate non-modeled work. That will require working with different levels of managers to understand what non-modeled work is being done. This work can be estimated or measured in many ways. If you have Six Sigma experts, involve them.

Managing resource capacity with PPM is an ongoing process, not a sudden shift to a computerized system. It will require planning and thought. In the beginning, the PPM resource information will be more valuable as a means of identifying problem areas and validating decisions than as a means of creating definitive budgeting recommendations. The good news is that what you create, even early on, doesn't have to be great to far surpass what most organizations have today. The big mistake is in thinking that a process that doesn't require ongoing discipline, planning, and refinement will meet your needs. If you don't have strong project planning processes, estimates of resource needs will always be suspicious.

One element that these steps leave out is the concept of buffers. Spending can be variable, in the same way that task durations and project completions can be variable. Unfortunately, most budgeting processes do not incorporate the "cost buffer" concept.[2] If you're stuck with single, un-buffered numbers in your budgets, you'll need to decide whether to give high or low estimates for resources. A high estimate for the coming year would involve putting padding back into tasks and observing the maximum probable resource requirements during the year. A low estimate would involve removing the padding and looking at the minimum probable resource needs. The buffer size would be some proportion (say, half) the difference between these estimates. Obviously high estimates cost more but minimize the chances of resource delays. Note that the use of cost buffers assumes that you have some flexibility in your spending. Where salaries are the major component of expenses, this means you can hire, fire, or transfer people in the time frame covered by the buffer. Otherwise, if the number of people remains the same, there is no conflict or tradeoff: you've got the people, so employ them where they'll be most useful.

Multi-Project Scheduling (Theory)

A set of independent schedules is almost always going to be unrealistic when those schedules share resources. Some resources will be over-booked. It may seem obvious that no organization should start more projects than it can work on without forcing people to multitask, but most project organizations don't have good means of figuring out how many projects to start. Therefore project starts are based, at best, on rules of thumb and gross estimates of what's possible, and thus tend to be aggressive.[3] Meanwhile, department budgets are kept at the minimum that's perceived to be necessary to meet current needs, where current needs include a great deal of multitasking. As a result of all this, resources tend to look very overloaded, especially the ones that are expensive, hard to hire, or hard to train.

Sometimes organizations say, "We dedicate resources to our projects." They do this in order to maximize project speed.[4] But in our experience, they still share a few resources; and the resources they share are often the most expensive and the most scarce. That means projects often wait for those resources to become available. In other words, *they maximize speed by dedicating the resources that have the least impact on speed.*

The standard critical chain approach to overloads on resources shared between projects is to pace the projects (sometimes known as "staggering") by pushing them out to the future based on the load on a particular resource known as the "pacing resource." This resource is sometimes called the "drum" resource, because it supplies the drumbeat to which the organization marches. The pacing resource is likely the most overloaded resource in the organization.[5] Figure 13.3 shows two project schedules, with the boxes and arrows

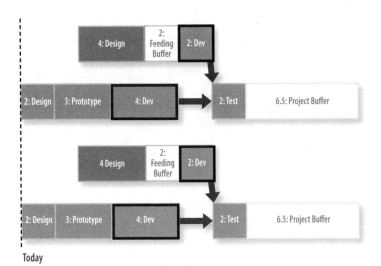

Today

Figure 13.3. Two project schedules

similar to those in figure 9.5. The number in each box represents a number of weeks duration and the name represents a resource. The dotted line represents the start of scheduling ("today") and the gold tasks are on the critical chain. We assume only one unit of the "Dev" resource and that Dev is most heavily loaded in this picture.

If we push the second project to the future so that there will be no resource conflict, we get figure 13.4. By pacing the second project, we have relieved the overload on Dev (see the bottom line of Dev tasks) and made both schedules more realistic. As time goes by, additional projects can be paced based on the pacing resource status of all the projects taken together.

A couple of questions often arise with this process. First, we haven't resolved contention across all resources. For example, in figure 13.4 the Design resource may be overloaded. The problem

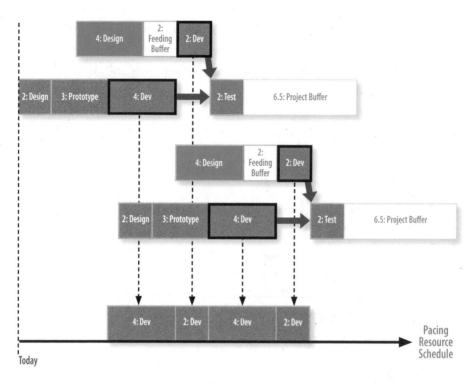

Figure 13.4. Two paced project schedules

is, if we adjust for every short-term overload on every resource, we'll be creating extra holes in our schedules, which will push our commitments out farther than we need to. The reality is that if on average Design has sufficient capacity, and if we know that the tasks won't happen exactly when we plan for them to happen, then we may as well not worry about leveling the Design resource, and instead allow the project buffers to absorb any small periods of unavailability. Meanwhile, we make sure that, on average, resources have the time they need by pacing the projects using the most overloaded resource; in this case, Dev.

Another potential problem is that fluctuations on tasks for the Dev resource may ripple through all projects in the organization, affecting commitments well into the future. The standard critical chain solution to this is called the "capacity buffer." Capacity is left open on the pacing resource between projects, so that the projects are essentially decoupled. We won't get into a detailed discussion here of how and when to use capacity buffers, except to note that ProChain Pipeline and Enterprise both support this concept through their "Reserved Capacity" features.

You'll note that this project pacing process requires setting and following priorities at the project portfolio level. This can be painful to initiate, but the alternative is to have unclear priorities and multitasking. Some organizations set project priorities only in order to decide how to pace the projects, and then assume that the pacing will allow them to finish everything. By assuming that all projects represent firm commitments and that resources have sufficient capacity to meet those commitments, people can avoid having to make further tradeoffs between projects. Instead, execution is simply a matter of prioritizing tasks according to the greatest impact on their respective project buffers. This approach can work well (for example, in organizations with many small projects), but when setting task priorities we usually recommend including some other factors, such as the relative priorities of projects.

Multi-Project Scheduling (Practice)

The previous section dealt with "critical chain theory" for multiple projects. Practice is somewhat more difficult. Earlier in this chapter we examined some problems with resource capacity modeling. Those problems aren't as severe with pacing, because you don't need information for as many resources; but the same problems exist. All the steps for managing capacity are also relevant for multi-project scheduling.

There's an additional problem that is quite vexing. In most cases we've encountered, the resource loads modeled in the schedules are not sufficient to cause any significant pacing of projects, no matter which resources you pick to pace with. In other words, based on your PPM schedules, resource-based pacing often has no impact at all.[6]

One response to this is to "stagger" project starts anyway; for example, by limiting the number of projects that may be worked on. This is called a "virtual drum." The major advantage of this is to minimize the opportunities for multitasking and thus speed the changes in behavior to create a non-multitasked world. It can help calm the Multitasking Maelstrom. A disadvantage is that this kind of limitation will seem arbitrary (in fact, it *is* arbitrary) and therefore lack credibility. Before jumping to any conclusions, it's worth looking at the two main reasons why standard pacing isn't normally effective.

First, as I've already noted, there are many things we normally don't model in critical chain schedules. That includes both non-project work and, in some cases, project work that just didn't seem important to include.

And second, our models are supposed to include unpadded, focused task durations. We're modeling the time we think resources will need in the new, single-tasked world. If everyone stopped multitasking and followed the models, chances are the projects in process *could* be worked without pacing.

I believe that in a command-and-control world with relatively small projects, either project pacing or the virtual drum can be applied fairly quickly and effectively. This would apply in job shops and various related manufacturing organizations, as well as in simpler design shops. You may even be able to "freeze" the introduction of new projects without having schedules for them, which—if properly managed—could reduce the potential for people to multitask, increase productivity, and result in a greater rate of project completion.

In a world of R&D, IT, or new product development projects, these techniques will be difficult because credibility of project plans is much more critical. Executives want some justification for "delaying" projects; others want to believe the plans before they agree to follow them. To be successful, you'll need to build your capacity picture for key resources, as already discussed. You should guide the organization to follow the six PPM principles. As you do this, you can use the critical chain tools such as capacity management and project pacing to provide input to your decision processes, while never forgetting that those inputs must be tempered with knowledge and experience. The more you have control over your projects and an understanding of your organization's capacity, the more you'll be able to rely on the results of the pacing process.

Tip

We have found it valuable to use the PPM pipeline tools to check the resource loads across multiple projects, even if the project planning isn't sufficiently mature to support pacing the projects. Examining loading in this way provides an important extra reality check for the project plans and the planned resource capacity.

Program Management

In PPM, a *program* is a very complex project with many components. It may make sense to schedule some of these components as *subprojects*. The presence of subprojects adds an extra dimension to the management of a project. Without subprojects, you may have a single project schedule with 10,000 or more tasks. With them, the complexity may be managed across several different project "entities."

Consider, for example, a drug development project at a company like Imventure. At a high level you might see multiple clinical trials, other types of studies, data analysis tasks, and various marketing efforts. The high-level project may have a few hundred high-level tasks, but each of these tasks might itself be a one- or two-year project. Aerospace, medical device, and other high tech programs can have similar levels of complexity.

The resource dimension of programs is also complex. Some resources may be shared across a program; others may be part of a resource organization that is relatively independent (or, in the case of vendors, completely independent). How many people do you need? What will be the impact of changes?

The difficulty in managing complex programs can by itself contribute significantly to the failure of large projects. It requires a great deal of work and a great deal of discipline to keep track of everything going on. The number of things you can't afford to mess up is proportionately greater in a more complex program. Meanwhile, planning is an exponential lever that works both ways: work you forgot to plan or do early on will have a proportionately greater effect later. The less experience an organization has in managing large projects, the more trouble they're likely to get into.

Planning and scheduling are important parts of program management, and PPM has mechanisms to help manage their complexity. The simplest way to schedule a program is to create a high-level schedule, with tasks representing subprojects. The subprojects can be managed separately by their own managers, with results passed back to the program manager. Sometimes a simple checklist is sufficient for a subproject; often it's important to build and manage a complete subproject plan. The structure of your planning, including the subprojects you create for a program, should reflect the existing organizational structure. For example, any subproject plan you create that isn't owned by a single "subproject manager" will have limited value.

When status information about subprojects is carried up to the program schedule, there can be discrepancies. For example, many times links don't go neatly from the finish of one component to the start of another. Sometimes there are links between tasks within components. ProChain Pipeline and Enterprise have mechanisms that enable you to use the PPM management process with virtually any kind of automatic links between and among programs and sub-projects. You can also represent resources that roll up to multiple schedules. For example, figure 13.5 shows a program-level schedule on the left and subprojects on the right. Inter-project connections are shown by gold boxes with arrows. The program-level schedule, inside the large black box on the left, has tasks (the smaller boxes) linked together. Two of its tasks (pointed to by large arrows) reference the subprojects on the right. In addition, a task in the upper subproject is referenced by a task in the lower subproject.

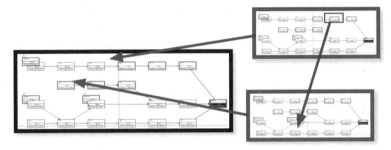

Figure 13.5. Program and subprojects

Use of subprojects requires extra discipline in how and when programs are updated. Usually meetings of the subproject teams are conducted the day before the program team meeting, in order to have the program status as up-to-date as possible. This high-lights the importance of "schedule design," the planning of how the schedule will be created and used.[7]

Multi-Project Communication

"Multi-Project Communication" includes many elements that affect many different people: task lists for people and groups that are working on several projects, the ability to update project information from anywhere in the world, multi-project dashboards, and so on. Essentially we're talking about enterprise-level communication of all project information—the PPM version of Enterprise Project Management. We've found that the larger and more spread out the organization, the more a web-based system like ProChain Enterprise (PCE) becomes indispensable.

Before looking at the technical aspects of the communication, it's important to highlight what exactly a system like PCE enables. Project teams can already have conference calls and update status without resorting to a new computer system. Project managers can already email status reports to senior managers. The basic capabilities are nothing new.

Two aspects to PCE are very important, especially if one is considering rolling PPM out to an organization. First is ongoing visibility. PPM shines a light into dark places. With PCE, the light is always on. If people know what they're supposed to do, and the information on whether or not they're doing it is visible, it becomes much more difficult not to do the right things. The principles become easier to follow, and it becomes more obvious when they're not being followed.

PPM shines light into dark places in many ways. Current task and project status is always visible. As key project tasks are delayed and we ask "why," we often find resource groups that are compulsively multitasking. Weak processes or poor compliance can be seen in fever charts through jumps in buffer consumption. Very often we find that important improvement initiatives—carefully targeted, properly paced initiatives—arise from a good project planning process. By the same token, sometimes other improvement initiatives are shown not to be terribly useful.

PCE also promotes both the language and behaviors of PPM. People will naturally gravitate toward the PPM approach if schedule-related team activities are centered around PCE information. If you try to adapt old systems to fit the new behaviors and language, there is a real risk that people will gravitate back to the old familiar ways of working.

Technically, PCE—along with other enterprise systems— enables real-time task and project updates from anywhere in the world. It enables various multi-project views of your project portfolio. For example, the multi-project fever chart shown in figure 13.6 allows you to view many projects at once, looking at both how far along the projects are (the horizontal dimension) and how much buffer has been consumed (the vertical dimension). PCE allows you to conduct 'what-if' exercises that help to figure out

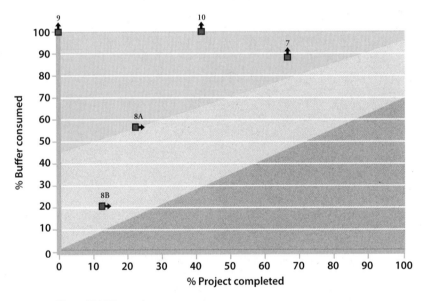

7   Gizmo 2000 Upgrade
8A   Gizmo 3000 — Demo at Trade Show
8A   Gizmo 3000 — Begin Production
9   Gizmo 4000
10   Widget Pro

Figure 13.6. Multi-project fever chart

resource needs and likely future project status. It pulls your project information together. But the technical capability has little value unless it's associated with a methodology that matches your needs. You need the processes to complement the tools.

Exercise

1. It is possible to take a top-down approach to implementing critical chain scheduling: create schedules as quickly as possible, cut task times unilaterally in order to create challenging schedules with time for buffers, and freeze project introductions (perhaps using a "virtual drum") to minimize multitasking and get people focused on moving projects through the system. Think through the likely advantages and disadvantages of this approach.[8]

14

PPM BEHAVIORS

The topic of "behaviors" could include everything that has to happen in an implementation. We have already discussed various principles and tools; critical chain scheduling contains implicit behaviors, as do buffer management and network building. In this chapter we review a few remaining types of behaviors before moving on to look at institutionalizing those behaviors.

The Project Updating Process

PPM project updating is a team effort. It is designed to accomplish the following objectives, based on the PPM principles:

- Ensure that the project schedule remains up-to-date and credible to both the entire project team and to senior management (Status, Ownership).
- Ensure that priorities and assignments are clear (Leverage, Priorities).
- Continue to plan ongoing buffer recovery and risk identification and mitigation efforts (Leverage, Planning).
- Track and evaluate remaining buffer (Status, Uncertainty).
- Make sure that people learn and practice the new language (Ownership).

A project update typically happens weekly, although it can be done more frequently. A particular sequence of actions, appropriate for a given project or organization, should be carried out at prescribed times, for example:

- Enter updates into ProChain Enterprise.
- Update buffer status according to those updates.
- Analyze the network to validate the updates and look for opportunities to address obstacles and speed the project up.
- Make needed changes to the project network.
- Send a status report to senior management. At a minimum, the status report should give them access to buffer status, key and upcoming tasks, major risks and mitigation strategies, and buffer recovery strategies.

Tip

The traditional task status value is "percent complete." If you want real status, collect instead the duration remaining; it is far clearer. If a four-day task was 25 percent complete on Tuesday and 40 percent complete on Thursday, when will it finish?

Tip

At really crucial times, project teams will sometimes do daily "standup" meetings in which they take five or ten minutes and talk about status of the current Check Tasks and how everyone can help.

One critical piece of the PPM updating process is the ongoing analysis, which involves using the project plan to evaluate different scenarios. Since this analysis is probably new for the project team, the project manager should take a strong leadership role so that analysis and buffer recovery discussions aren't shortchanged. However, the team should quickly get to a point where everyone participates.

Another critical piece is the report to management. We usually have teams produce a weekly status report, created through ProChain Enterprise, that is sent to management via email. That way everyone knows the oversight is there, even if management doesn't study the report in detail. Many times, we also use the kind of Checklist Survey shown in figure 12.2 to make sure teams establish an agenda for buffer updates and stick with it. The results of that Checklist Survey, collected weekly, are then put into a histogram like that shown in figure 12.3 to give to senior management.

While we typically update projects weekly, we rarely *reschedule* them. That is, we recalculate buffer status, including the impact chain, but we don't recalculate the buffer sizes or locations. A full reschedule can be disruptive, potentially moving the project's finish line, dramatically changing the fever chart picture and shifting task priorities. It should only be done when the current picture is no longer realistic, which means when we think the project has a good chance of completing outside the span of the project buffer—either before the start of the project buffer or after its finish.

Risk Management

Risk management has a standard vocabulary that includes concepts such as risk, mitigation, contingency, and so on. It's a great idea to identify your major risks and create risk mitigation and contingency plans for them. While the details of risk management processes are outside the scope of this book, four common issues associated with risk management are worth mentioning here. First, very often risks and associated plans are put together and then ignored. People have trouble devoting time to risk management. Therefore I recommend spending a few minutes of your

weekly Project Update meetings to review risks and their corresponding mitigation and contingency plans.

Second, people often try to identify and handle too many small
risks. This diffuses focus from the few really important risks. The
presence of buffers in a project schedule means that you can put more
emphasis on the high-probability, high-impact risks where it belongs
and ignore the details. Figure out which risks could cause significant
buffer consumption, then let the buffers sweat the small stuff.

The third issue is a simple technical point: often the listed risks
aren't really risks. People talk about the outcome as the risk, which
makes the risk a little more difficult to think about constructively.
For example, from a risk management perspective it would be inac-
curate to say, "There is a risk that our project will be held up due
to vendor delays." Instead, say, "There is a risk of vendor delays,
which would cause the project to be held up." The risk is the event
that may or may not occur, the vendor delays. The potential impact
is a consequence of the risk, the project delay. We're going to miti-
gate the vendor delays, and maybe put together contingency plans
so that even if they occur the project won't be delayed as much.

Last but not least, risks can represent positives—opportunities,
for example, to speed up the project. "If this were to happen, the
project would be completed more quickly." Evaluating key tasks
and dollars of value per day saved, how do we maximize the chances
that such happy risks will come to pass?

> ### EXAMPLE
>
> One company needed to complete a group of 130 projects within a
> year; it was crucial to their financial viability. The group performing
> most of the work did a great job creating critical chain schedules and
> getting the work through their area. The projects would have been

completed in a year, except that a downstream group, although identified as a risk early in the process, was not ready and became a severe
bottleneck. There were two solutions that could have been employed:
either include that downstream group in the planning and execution
process, or employ better risk management.

Relay Race and Work Rules

The PPM principles are fairly high-level, as we saw already in the
pyramid of figure I.4. You can't just give them to someone and
expect big changes; they need to be coupled with understanding
and mentoring in the associated tools and behaviors. Earlier, we
looked at the project updating process. That discussion contained
several examples of behaviors at the project level.

There are also behaviors that need to be practiced at the functional group level—behaviors that can reinforce one another if practiced consistently or that can interfere with the PPM efforts if done
poorly. For example, when people have work they absolutely need to
finish quickly, they will usually find a quiet place where they won't
be interrupted in order to get it done. They will inevitably follow a
relay race model, running as quickly as possible until they can hand
off the baton. Similarly, when a project is both very urgent and very
important, an organization can communicate that message to all
the workers and complete the project remarkably quickly. We can
all think of examples; the United States would never have achieved
the goal of sending a man to the moon by 1969 without attaching
a great deal of urgency and importance to it.

The challenge of PPM, and one of its huge benefits, is to make
that relay race the norm so that all projects are completed quickly.
We find it useful to use the relay race analogy to explain PPM

to team members. Those with the baton (key tasks) should move ahead as quickly as possible; others should help them do that. The longer key tasks sit around, the slower the race will be run.

Making the relay race real normally requires significant changes in the ways people carry out their work. A milestone system such as Imventure's, for example, produces train schedules—immovable,

TABLE 3	Work rules	

"TRAIN SCHEDULE" WORK RULES	"RELAY RACE" WORK RULES
Start tasks as soon as you can; hand off when it is time.	Start initial "gating" tasks on or after their projected times, unless those times are overridden by the project manager. Start non-gating tasks when ready. Hand off tasks when done.
Switch between tasks as needed. Don't hesitate to interrupt others for something important to you.	Avoid task switching and interruptions: work tasks to their handoffs or logical stopping points before moving on.
Use your milestones to determine what needs to be worked most urgently.	Prioritize tasks according to their impact on the project buffers.
"Done" is next Tuesday, ready or not. Hit your milestones.	Find out what you need to know, including priorities and what really constitutes "done."
Avoid reporting task status until the milestone date is reached.	Help everyone to focus on completing the key tasks, and hence the project, quickly. Report task status when finished, and at least weekly.
As far as possible, accommodate all requests, especially from people above you in the organization.	Practice saying "no", "not now" or "yes, however," and explaining why.
Look out for number one.	Help projects finish more quickly; help one another to create a better work environment.

sacred due dates—that do not promote early completion. One way to express the functional-level behaviors is as "work rules." Table 3 gives some examples of bad ("train schedule") and good ("relay race") work rules.

"Gating tasks" were mentioned in Chapter 9; they are tasks with no predecessors. PPM schedules gating tasks to start as late as possible, taking into account buffers. That helps to ensure that the work does not sit around longer than necessary. There are often advantages to having gating tasks start later—such as delaying expenditures or minimizing rework—as long as they don't start so late that they delay the project.

Many different kinds of work rules can be created; the specific rules one should use, and means of implementing them, depend greatly on the organization and the specific functional area. Some people like to put a red chain on their door to indicate work on key tasks and say, "Don't interrupt me." An extreme case is 5S as practiced by just-in-time manufacturing organizations.[1]

You can teach people and you can mentor them, but every process will eventually stop working unless it contains a mechanism for self-improvement. In the case of functional groups, one such mechanism is the regular staff meeting. If people meet regularly and discuss the work rules—how they relate to the principles and how to follow them—the rules can improve and people can learn better how to follow them. If people have no such discussion, the rules become—or remain—someone else's. People must take ownership of the process. They will do that if the process benefits them. The process will benefit them if they have a say in how it works.

The Language of PPM

Learning a new skill—like PPM—is like learning a new language. You have to learn the words, you have to learn how words work together to communicate thoughts, and you have to practice to become fluent. And it isn't nearly as useful if you're the only one who speaks that language.[2]

Chapter 8 introduced the idea of the "vocabulary of uncertainty." In fact, there are vocabulary elements associated with each principle and each tool. Sometimes the words are new, but more often they're old with new meanings. That means it's easy to become confused, because people assume they already know what you mean. Here are some terms that we use to talk about the PPM principles:

- **Ownership**: vision, message
- **Leverage**: lever, constraint, critical chain, impact chain, pacing resource
- **Priorities**: multitasking, single-tasking, sequence, focus, percent task impact, subordination
- **Status**: remaining duration, done, buffer consumption
- **Planning**: task, resource, duration, buffer size, project, program, portfolio
- **Uncertainty**: project buffer, feeding buffer, focused duration, low-risk duration, commitment date, stretch goal, probability

Lack of vocabulary doesn't completely disable thinking. However, it does inhibit our ability to formulate, analyze, and communicate ideas. Available vocabulary also guides the direction of thoughts. We tend to think and talk about things we're familiar with. We tend to search for common language when meeting other people. If you're discussing project status and everyone is most familiar with milestones, that's the language you'll tend to use.

One of the fundamental shifts in using PPM—indeed, in using most new processes—is in learning the new language. That requires not just classroom learning, but field experience. You can't learn a new language without practice in hearing, speaking, and thinking it. That means you need to be around other people who are also using the new language.

Often, a critical chain implementation will start with some dramatic successes. However, if the implementation is not well planned, key people may not internalize the new language. Those who use it well have to make accommodation for those who don't. Eventually, the new meanings get subverted and the old ways reassert themselves. People may continue to use the new words, but only to express the old concepts. "How much buffer do you have?" for example, may come to mean, "How much slack between now and your milestone date?"

Resistance to Change

If we've done a good job creating schedules, they will be great tools for measurement and communication. However, there can also be resistance to use of the schedules. Authors cite many reasons for "resistance to change": fear of the unknown, lack of training, investment in the status quo, and so on.[3] Many of the typical reservations people express are excuses, because their real reservations would be uncomfortable to express. "Resistance to change" is a convenient category that often lets us off the hook: there's nothing we can do, people are just resistant.

What we perceive as resistance to change typically comes from a couple of major considerations. First, there is a minimum by which benefits must outweigh costs. In today's world, people are constantly trying to sell things to one another: relationships, used cars, hair products, political candidates, and so on.[4] That makes us inherently skeptical about sales, and sets the bar fairly high as we weigh benefits and costs.[5]

People often perceive the net value of a change to be negative. That may happen, for example, when they don't experience urgency or when they don't see the value for themselves. It's very easy to say that PPM makes sense for an organization, but a resource manager may decide that for them the negatives far outweigh the positives.

They will "resist" the change. By the same token, any time you try to implement something that has no perceived value for key individuals, you'll find success to be an uphill struggle. Meanwhile, recognizing your enthusiasm, they may be completely unwilling to confess that they don't see the value; so from your point of view they just look resistant.

People may perceive changes to be negative for various less-than-obvious reasons having to do with their perceived personal costs and benefits:

- People resist visibility into what's going on, because what's going on violates many common-sense principles. For example, nobody would argue that Schedule Chicken makes any sense for a company, and yet some places it's pervasive.
- Good project (or milestone) managers are usually adept at keeping some time reserves hidden, in order to protect them-selves in case of problems. The critical chain approach seeks to make that protection explicit, changing a system that seems to be working—*for them*—into a system that works for everyone.
- PPM can challenge other competing initiatives, both new initiatives waiting for funding and existing initiatives that still haven't delivered what was promised. Many times people hitch their careers to initiatives, and un-hitching them from failed initiatives is a painful process.

The second consideration that can cause resistance to change is a belief that change is impossible. Often, people have seen so many management initiatives come and go—many trying to instill com-mon-sense principles—that they've become immune. The general reaction is: if we close our eyes and wait, it'll go away; meanwhile, we have real work to do. People can be convinced in many ways that change is possible; piloting and mentoring relationships will be discussed later in this book.[6]

Instead of expressing their real concerns, people often use excuses. For example, critical chain scheduling frequently receives the criticism that "it's not new." If you break PPM or critical chain into pieces, the pieces aren't new. The same could be said of a painting or a protein molecule. The combination of pieces and their relationships is crucial. PPM is a combination of critical chain project scheduling and other tools, designed to create practical results for real organizations. The combination produces the results and PPM represents a new combination. On the other hand, this may be one excuse that we can safely agree with and then ignore. Consider this quote: "Looking back on the stages by which various fresh ideas gained acceptance, it can be seen that the process was eased when they could be presented, not as something radically new, but as the revival in modern times of a time-honoured principle or practice that had been forgotten."[7]

Real sources of resistance can be overcome in many ways. A detailed list is far beyond the scope of this book, but three important concepts are discussed in the next chapter. You need selling, because people need to buy the change. You need marketing in order to help people look at the implementation in a positive light. You need feedback loops in order to build perception of value, to build trust, and to make sure things stay on track.

Exercises

1. How many races can a single person run at the same time?
2. What is the impact of each of the work rules in table 3 on the PPM principles? Consider both the Train Schedule and Relay Race work rules.
3. What is the language you use in your organization today for each of the six PPM principles?

4. Quickly list ten reasons you've heard people give to explain their resistance to a change. Don't hesitate to include friends and family members. How many are reasons and how many are excuses?

15

CHANGE AND THE
CYCLE OF RESULTS

There are many aspects and viewpoints regarding changing organizational behaviors and cultures, and much has been written on the subject. This chapter describes some of the concepts I've found to be important in changing to PPM.

"Organization change" ultimately comes down to individuals. You must change, I must change, everyone in our group must change. However, the biggest problem we face with a good improvement methodology like PPM isn't changing how one person works. With appropriate training and mentoring, most people—whether project managers, project teams, or leadership groups—will come fairly quickly to understand the value for them in PPM.

The problem is change across many people, in a synchronized way. Most improvement processes start with a few evangelists. They promote, wheedle, and cajole; after much hard work, they sometimes get permission to take their solution more broadly. But no such group can effectively train or mentor 1,000 (or 10,000 or 100,000) people in an organization in any reasonable time frame. Thus to implement, they typically give the organization new systems, measurements, and training, and hope this will be sufficient. That is a little like taking a balloon, blowing it up, and letting it go, hoping it will hit a particular spot on the wall. No matter how well you aim, it could go anywhere. So after implementing, the next step is to spend a phenomenal amount of work getting the balloon moving in the right direction.[1]

Obviously the balloon must be properly filled and aimed; or, to jump out of the metaphor, the implementation must be resourced and chartered. But you must also establish channels to guide the implementation, and make sure those channels are used. The more you can track and guide, the better your chances of success.

Part of this tracking and guidance comes from effective tools and processes. In addition, three major elements are needed (and often overlooked) in trying to guide an implementation to success: sales, marketing, and feedback loops.

Sales and Marketing

My personal definition of selling is "getting someone to do something." That may mean they do something for the first time; it may mean they continue doing something. For a PPM implementation, we're ultimately selling various kinds of behaviors. Furthermore, we're not looking for people to buy a change once; we're looking for them to buy it many times, over and over into the future.[2]

To buy, people must have some sort of *urgency* that causes them to do something differently in the first place. Otherwise they'll find many reasons (or excuses) why they shouldn't be doing it. That urgency can be established through personal relationships; it can come from the boss saying, "Do it now;" and it can come from the market saying, "Change or die." The *type* of urgency will be different depending on the person and the situation. There is also a minimum *level* of urgency needed to cause anything to happen.

"Buying" an implementation—the flip side of selling it—must also provide people with *value*. If they see a net positive value to doing something, they will continue doing it. If not, getting them to continue will be a lot of work.[3] If project managers don't see value to themselves in planning, they won't do it.

You won't find this in a marketing book, but my definition of marketing is "getting people to feel a particular way about something." As any change process begins, people will make assumptions and develop opinions, whether those assumptions and opinions have a factual basis or not. Many times skepticism will be based on past experience rather than on what the implementation is or what value it might provide. For example, as we start a PPM implementation we frequently hear people say, "Here we go again, another flavor of the month." The purpose of marketing PPM is to give people a good foundation for valid opinions, without having to mentor each individual. Naturally, a "good foundation" means we'll express our message in a positive way. That goes back to a point made earlier: chances are, if people believe an implementation will succeed, it will; if they don't, it won't.[4]

The good opinions created by marketing can also help to create social pressure. As more and more people see the value in doing something, more and more people will jump on board.[5] The trick is then to make sure that when they jump, they're properly prepared.

Marketing can be done much more broadly than selling, because it can be accomplished with less direct effort. Good marketing must prepare people for buying later on. It's therefore a critical element of any large implementation.

Feedback Loops

As you implement, there will be times when things go well and inevitably times when things go wrong. Sometimes you will feel like you're on a roller coaster. Maybe a key person leaves, a project team already has strong ideas about scheduling, or new products have technical problems. All these can divert focus. How do you know when and how to change course when things go wrong?

"Feedback loop" is a term that encompasses several elements under the heading of "see what's happening and fix what's wrong."

The obvious meaning is making course corrections based on real data. Buffer management provides feedback. Several other mechanisms were discussed in Chapter 12, "Measuring Success." The more you can check what's happening, compare it with what should be happening, and make corrections, the easier it will be to keep projects of all types on track.

Another important type of feedback loop is the "Cycle of Results." It's a process of feedback to individuals or groups, to make sure expectations are on track and that positive trust is built. I believe the Cycle of Results, in some form, is essential for any significant change initiative, including PPM. It is described in the remainder of this chapter.

Show Me the Value

Imagine two virtually identical families, the Abels and the Bakers, who live in virtually identical houses in virtually identical neighborhoods in the same town. Each family has decided that it needs a new porch.

Mrs. Abel calls A-to-Z Contractors and says she needs a new porch. Mr. Z, who takes the call for A-to-Z, says that they can start immediately. A-to-Z comes out the next day and begins building the porch. A week later, Mr. Z gives Mrs. Abel a bill for $10,000.

Mrs. Baker instead calls Alpha-Omega Builders and says she needs a new porch. Mr. Omega, who takes the call, asks why she needs a porch, and discovers that the old one is falling apart. "I told Henry," Mrs. Baker says, "that one day someone is going to put a foot through the porch and sue us for everything we're worth. I don't want to be around when that happens, I'll tell you right now."

Mr. Omega comes out to the house and talks with the Bakers about how to build the reliable porch they need. They go over materials, color, style, location, and so on. They spend several hours going over designs, look, and durability. They talk about how the workmen will operate, building permits, and scheduling. Mr. Omega gives the Bakers a quote and they agree on the spot to move forward. The next day, Alpha-Omega shows up and begins working. Throughout the process, Mr. Omega periodically explains to Mrs. Baker what's going on; a week later, the porch is finished. Before Mr. Omega hands the bill for $10,000 to Mrs. Baker, he walks around the porch with her, explaining to her what they've done and making sure that it matches the specifications they agreed to. He explains their ten-year guarantee and tells her to be sure to call him if they have any problems.

There's one more thing that's important to understand in this story: the porches that end up being built are, for all practical purposes, identical. They have the same materials, same style, same guarantee; everything is the same.

Given this background, answer the question, "**Which porch is better?**"

Admittedly, the question isn't fair. It can't be answered with the data given. And that by itself is important to think about: functionally identical porches, very similar families, and *one porch may be better.*

What might be different?

First, Alpha-Omega and Mrs. Baker put more time into their porch. So, in a sense, it cost them more. That is a consideration that can't be ignored.

Second, Mr. Omega built ownership in the porch by working with Mrs. Baker. He helped her set expectations; he adapted to her needs; he validated that the needs were met. By the end, there was no reason for Mrs. Baker to suppose that her porch was anything other than exactly what she wanted.

Third, we don't know for sure what Mrs. Abel agreed to. It's very possible that she was surprised by the final price or by any number of other aspects of the porch. *We don't know.* And if we don't know, Murphy's Law suggests that there will be a problem.

For example: it could be that Mrs. Abel was surprised by the appearance of the porch, and therefore not happy with it. If she can't fully enjoy it, it's quite possible that Mr. Abel can't either. This could lead to additional costs in having the porch modified. One might expect that the Bakers, on the other hand, love their porch. Given that it's exactly what they wanted, one would expect them to use it frequently for family events, parties, and just sitting quietly in the evening sipping mint juleps.

In short, it's possible that the Bakers' porch is significantly better by any of a number of criteria. It may be more functional. If Mrs. Abel really hates her porch, it could even be longer-lasting. The Bakers' porch is also likely to get their vendor follow-on business. The porches are physically identical, and *we don't know which is better. We do know, however, that the Bakers' porch is just what they wanted.*

If the Bakers' porch is better, it's because they were sold a solution to their problem, they knew it was a solution to their problem, and Mr. Omega verified that it was and would continue to be a solution to their problem. In that case, by managing perceptions and expectations, the communication process itself created significant value—value that had nothing directly to do with the physical product purchased or with any training on how to use that product. The transfer of information back and forth, with the trust and ownership that resulted, gave the Bakers confidence in their purchase. In addition, because of this trust and confidence, the Bakers are more likely to use Alpha-Omega in the future and recommend them to their friends. And why not, if they got a porch that perfectly fit their needs?

With critical chain consulting, I have seen both A-to-Z implementers and Alpha-Omega implementers. Some people just come in and do their training and facilitation; others spend time communicating expectations and results. Which approach someone uses is typically a matter of personal inclination rather than conscious choice. We've found that when consultants—internal or external—

make the effort to learn about a client's problems and help the client solve them, when they communicate and plan, the results tend to be very good. When they perform the technical implementation without the communication, the results tend to be poor. The Alpha-Omega approach, in our business, is usually much better.

Are you an A-to-Z implementer, or an Alpha-Omega implementer?

Let's look at the elements of successful communication, and then relate them to a PPM implementation.

The Cycle of Results

The communication process we're talking about is called the "Cycle of Results" or CORE™. It's really just an expansion on the old "tell them what's going to happen, make it happen, and confirm that it happened." In other words, set expectations, deliver, and show that you've delivered. This is a standard recipe for writing books, doing business, and communicating. The basic process is shown in figure 15.1.

The boxes represent existing states or "things that have been generated." Actions are shown on the arrows. The arrows represent time sequence. For example: plan and create ownership before implementing; set expectations before obtaining commitment. You might read this as, "If you have urgency, you can describe a vision in order to set expectations. If you have set expectations, you can plan and create ownership in order to create commitment." And so on.

Everything revolves around the sense of **urgency**, also called the "burning platform." There must be something that needs doing or fixing *now*. Urgency is the enemy of procrastination. Urgency can come from physical reality ("quit smoking or die of emphysema"), it can be manufactured by management (anything from "here are the benefits you'll get" to "management is providing the tools and

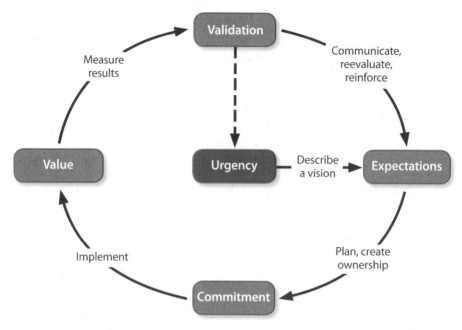

Figure 15.1. Cycle of Results

commitment to make this happen" to "your bonus depends on hitting this target date" to "fix project management or we'll outsource IT"), it can be internally generated ("I am not happy in my job"), or it can be some combination ("pressure to hit the back-to-school market window is causing me a lot of stress").[6] The urgency of the Bakers came from a concern that someone might get hurt. Notice that Mr. Omega asked explicitly what was driving the Bakers' desire to have a new porch; that allowed him to have discussions about what was important to the Bakers.

Urgency must be owned by the people who need to change. For example, if Mr. Baker had a sense of urgency about building a porch, it may have been the same as his wife's, driven by a concern for their guests; it may have been driven solely by a desire to keep his wife happy. Any of these might be specific to cause him to take action. Note that urgency is normally specific to individuals, so it's not really correct to talk about "organizational urgency." A CEO may care about project speed because her bonus depends on it; the average worker may not care about speed at all. It's also important to distinguish between the type of urgency (e.g. project speed) and the level (e.g. how much the CEO cares about her bonus).

Managers often rank their people's level of urgency as "high," because the manager has said something was urgent. This frequently doesn't translate to real urgency for people, because no measurable results are expected and consequently people have no reason to take ownership. This is one reason that middle management, used to inhabiting the "Zone of Reconciliation," will continue to try to maintain the status quo. It shouldn't be surprising that nothing changes until the urgency is made real for them.

From an understanding of people's urgency, we can describe a **vision** of the future we are trying to create. This vision should be common to those touching or touched by the implementation, because we will be working with and synchronizing people performing many different roles. The vision could be described as the story of how we expect the organization to change. This story must be meaningful to the people we are working with, related to their urgent need, and shared by the people who must change. Ideally, it will be a positive vision that people can embrace.

Although the pain and urgency may be different for different people, the vision—the picture that shows people addressing their urgency—should be the same. It is a unifying force. A specific implementation may address multiple problems and provide many forms of value, even though the vision is described in a common way.

In describing the vision to different parties—in describing what will be different, and in relating the vision to their pain and urgency—we set **expectations** for the implementation: what concrete actions will be taken, what results we expect, when we expect those results. Keep in mind that the expectations an individual will care about—in other words, what they will remember—is the value of the changes to them: their personal benefits minus their cost. In setting expectations, we haven't actually obtained a commitment from anyone that they will change something. But we do have agreement at this point that change makes sense, and we have some common understanding of what it will look like.

The next action is to **plan** the implementation. What tasks shall we carry out: training, software installation, schedule building? Whose behaviors will change, to what? Key thought leaders in the organization must be involved in the planning process. They will contribute significant value to the plan, and their support—their **commitment**—is much more likely if they have some **ownership** of the actions and results. Mrs. Abel had less ownership in her porch, because Mr. Z didn't involve her in the planning process.

For a PPM implementation, the planning and ownership may lead to other actions. For example, management may need to change policies regarding the assignment of personnel or the establishment of commitment dates. Minimally we want to get to the point where key thought leaders are committed to the vision. If the vision is meaningful to them and we can deliver results on the vision, we can get their commitment to making it work.

The next action, **implementation**, is the area where we typically focus most of our time and attention. This is where A-to-Z spent all their effort. It is important to understand that the implementation is not just a set of tasks; it should be a coherent approach to producing **value**. This value should address the pain and urgency we have identified. Those for whom the implementation does not produce value will not care about its success.

In order to see if everyone did what they said they would do, and to make sure the effects were as expected, we must **measure** the results on an ongoing basis. Very often, as we start an implementation, there are many activities taking place and many fires to fight. It's tempting to start without collecting data. But doing so would be a huge mistake. Unless we begin measuring from the starting point, it is very difficult to show that we have accomplished what we promised. Could Mr. Z have convinced Mrs. Abel that he had done exactly what she wanted, when he hadn't collected initial data or set expectations? Wherever possible, we need to collect baseline information so that we can compare performance today with performance tomorrow. With results measured, we can **validate** what we think we've achieved. Without them, we can't.

These results must be collected and they must be **communicated**. Whenever we set expectations, we must close the loop and make sure both that the expectations were met and that the people whose expectations we set *know* that they were met. Mrs. Baker knew her expectations were met because she talked them through with Mr. Omega. Here are a few things that happen if we *don't* communicate:

- Rumors and misleading information grow.
- Consultants assume that results are good.
- People assume that results don't need to be validated or communicated.

The net result is miscommunication that can lead to damaged relationships. You have a worse porch.

Communication must go both ways, input and output. If we only send, or only receive, we are not communicating. Even in a training course, the instructor should be alert to what the students are feeling. Collecting the data and validating the value will often give us useful tips on what is and isn't important in an implementation. As we talk with people, we should listen for answers to various questions: What do they see as valuable? Do they care about the things we expected them to care about? Are there new obstacles that need to be addressed? By communicating, we constantly **reinforce** and **reevaluate**, for ourselves and for others.

This communication process will, in turn, result in revisions to the **expectations**. Maybe things will happen more quickly; maybe they will take longer. Maybe new tasks have become necessary in order for the implementation to be more successful. By communicating results and revising expectations, we close the loop, reinforcing people's understanding and involvement. By managing expectations and delivering on them, we build trust.

Figure 15.1 shows a dotted line from "Validation" to "Urgency." Sometimes during the course of an implementation we gather information that invalidates our original assumptions. For example, we may be told that predictability is essential to management, but we discover that in reality predictability is in all cases trumped by cost. That means if our vision doesn't relate to cost and cost reductions, our chances of real success are dramatically reduced. We may need to modify the sense of urgency, the vision, expectations, and so on as we learn more.

Applying the Cycle of Results

Implementing PPM should result in behavior changes across an entire organization; and an organization might have anywhere from under 10 to more than 100,000 people. Chances are we won't be able to apply PPM everywhere directly, certainly not all at once. So where should we begin applying the Cycle of Results?

We start with the key stakeholders for the implementation. These are people whose commitment is make-or-break for the implementation. That normally includes senior management (the Steering Team), PMO staff, and implementation sponsors. How do we work with these people? The basic approach is as follows:

- Identify the key stakeholders for the implementation.
  These are people who care directly about the success of the

implementation, or people whose lack of support could result in obstacles.

- Learn about the organization. Talk with key stakeholders about their pain, their urgency, and their vision for a solution. Find out what kind of change PPM is likely to create.
- Create and describe a shared vision for the implementation.
- Set expectations with key stakeholders. They need to understand their costs, benefits, and risks.
- Work with key stakeholders to create an implementation plan.
- Perform the implementation work.
- Constantly measure and validate results.
- Feed back results at all stages, making sure that what you are doing is producing value for people.
- Adapt the processes to maximize the value.

Notice that these steps essentially follow the Cycle of Results process. In addition, people inside the organization should adopt the Cycle of Results model and follow it when communicating; our experience shows that this dramatically reduces the bumps they'll experience in the implementation road. This is the ideal implementation environment, a truly change-ready organization.

Exercises

1. Examine a large improvement initiative that you currently have going on. List the types and levels of urgency different people currently have that will help to move it forward. How much real ownership has been built up? What chances do you give of long-term success for this initiative?
2. Think through which of the elements of figure 15.1 relate to sales, marketing, or feedback loops.

INSTITUTIONALIZING
PPM

How do you institutionalize a methodology? How do you make it part of the DNA of an organization, so that there is no longer a question of whether or not to do it? Some important elements of institutionalization for PPM are described in this chapter.

Processes

Most large organizations have great respect for processes: processes for job reviews, for designing software, for building new plants, even for changing culture. The injection of government processes—environmental, procurement, drug approval, etc.—add extra levels of difficulty to projects. Many times processes are frustrating for the people involved, because they periodically force people to do things that seem nonsensical or even counter-productive.

Despite the pain, a growing business must have processes for key business elements. Process is a form of knowledge management. It means people don't have to re-invent approaches that are frequently repeated. It means certain expectations are given in certain situations and don't have to be reset over and over. It means even those new to a company can quickly reach a minimum level of competence in working with their colleagues. In short, while standard processes can sometimes seem like a sort of fossilization, they are also a means of synchronization.

This leads to a common "process conflict"—create more processes, in order to better synchronize how people work together; versus create fewer or less rigorous processes, in order to remain more flexible. Another similar conflict is to follow all process steps, in order to conform to existing knowledge of "best practices;" versus bypassing process steps, because they don't add value. Many times people break this conflict unilaterally, bypassing process steps by rationalizing that they don't add value. If they truly understand the given process well enough to do this, that probably implies a need to modify the process: defining the conditions under which a particular step or process isn't needed.

It's especially important to follow processes when transferring a methodology like PPM, because students will not have their mentor's intuitive understanding. When process steps are bypassed, students may learn that those steps are optional, without learning how to evaluate *when* they're optional.

The business literature contains many discussions of processes.[1] It's important to think through how you set up and adapt your processes in order to capture the value in using processes while avoiding the drawbacks.

From a project management perspective, certain processes are essential. Change control, project approval, project scheduling, and project close-out are all very important processes in the new product development world. The PPM process used for single project scheduling has three major phases (Prepare, Plan, and Execute) with many individual steps inside. In addition, there is an ongoing "Learn" phase that includes data collection, assessment, and improvement. That implies that we actively collect information and improve the process as experience is gained.

While any individual process or process element could be considered a tool, the concept and importance of Process is an attitude and a behavior. If you believe in learning and in codifying that learning so that others can capitalize on it, you will create and adapt processes. You have a Process attitude. If you would rather that people figure out how to deal with situations anew each time they arise, you do not have that attitude.[2]

> ## EXAMPLE
>
> Electronics Systems[3] is a US-based $250 Million subsidiary of a large multinational conglomerate. They design and manufacture electronic controls used in various industrial applications.
>
> When William Morton started as VP of R&D, the R&D area was widely regarded as a big problem. He quickly realized that they didn't just need new tools or software; they needed a full set of product development processes.
>
> Over the next three years, with some outside help, Morton implemented many essential processes, including project phases and gates, critical chain scheduling, and capacity planning. The end results: by the third year, all projects were completing on-time or early, and the reduction in multitasking had significantly improved both productivity and the quality of work life.

PMO and Certification

On the surface, the fundamental PPM concepts appear fairly simple. How hard could it be to implement critical chains, buffers, or single-tasking? Because of this, people often assume that a few hours of training will be sufficient.

The reality is that the methodology needed to implement PPM is quite complex. Some of that complexity can be removed by tailoring it to fit the environment, but ultimately changing people's behavior takes repetition over time.[4] Without this, people will revert to behaviors they're most comfortable with. In addition, obstacles need to be overcome, and not everything can be planned in advance.

Part of the goal of an organization-wide implementation of PPM (a "rollout") is to transfer ownership of the PPM process from consultants (internal or external) to the organization. Typically a Project Management Office (PMO, also known as a Program Management Office) owns PPM for the organization. The PMO is responsible for maintaining and evolving the methodology to meet the organization's changing needs. A discussion of how to start up a PMO is beyond the scope of this book, but one thing that's very important is a charter that clearly describes PMO responsibilities and measurements. Don't set out on this journey without having a reasonable idea of where you want to go.

We like to apply the rigorous "Prochain Expert Certification" process, so that we're sure the PMO includes several individuals who are fully qualified to use, teach, and mentor the different elements of PPM. These PPM Experts are preferably capable facilitators well respected in the organizations they'll be working with. They need to teach courses, facilitate various kinds of planning sessions, make needed changes to the methodology, implement those changes, and train new experts. An organization invests a great deal in its ProChain experts and expects a great deal in return.

Expert Certification involves both oral exams and significant mentoring to teach the needed practical skills. Certification candidates are assigned mentors who guide them through the PPM launch process (and any other relevant processes, including implementation and multi-project). This is the only way we know of to make sure that PPM experts are qualified to do what they need to do.

Steering Team

The senior-level Steering Team is a critical element of any PPM implementation.[5] This group of executives is responsible and ultimately accountable for making sure the implementation stays on track. They must approve and nurture the vision for the implementation.

Very often the question arises, "Suppose I've lined up my boss's boss's boss, what exactly am I going to ask him to do? He doesn't care about schedules." The Steering Team has a few major jobs. First is to use their positions—and the visibility and authority that come with them—to promote or "sell" the new approach. This implies, above all, using the new language. They need to show that the organization and its management are serious about this change effort; in a sense, they need to be able to "talk the talk."[6] They should ask to see and discuss buffer reports. It's also useful to set up company-wide "town hall" meetings to talk about the importance of the PPM initiative and address concerns directly.

Very often, large organizations spend millions of dollars on new management technologies and then tell people, "Use this if you want to." This means people never get a solid message that this is the direction the organization is going. Even with a good methodology, such as PPM, this will result in implementations that take much longer than necessary and produce fewer benefits. People need to be accountable, not just for results but also for a common language. Sooner or later, the message needs to be simply, "Do it this way."

The Steering Team's second major job is to help overcome obstacles when they arise. The Steering Team may need to make certain resources available or get certain people to move their behinds.

Third is to keep an eye on how well the implementation is going and take action if they see problems. This is especially important after the consultants leave.

There's a fourth, more difficult element to the Steering Team's job. Very often, the PPM planning process sheds a light on systemic problems or "opportunities for improvement." For example, a lack of process knowledge in certain resource groups, poor management, or a critical shortage of a particular resource may be exposed by PPM's systematic project scheduling and analysis process. These opportunities should be seized by the Steering Team to gain ongoing improvements.

Steering Teams don't make a big time commitment, but they do have a discipline commitment. They generally meet once a month, sometimes as part of another meeting (like a staff or portfolio meeting). The meetings will initially include training; then it's a matter of communicating status and giving or receiving feedback on the implementation. While consultants may communicate PPM results to the Steering Team, that communication will ultimately be the responsibility of the PMO and the PMO director.

Sometimes Steering Team members *don't* do these things. The first reason is lack of time, which means lack of priority for the implementation. People must absolutely be respectful of executives' time, but beyond that, if executives can't find the time needed to help make an implementation successful, the implementation is probably a bad idea. Second is lack of awareness or understanding. Creating awareness and understanding are big reasons for having Steering Team meetings.

The least understood, and therefore potentially most dangerous, reason that executives don't properly support implementations is lack of appreciation for the critical importance of their authority. An executive may say, "I'm not going to tell people to do this; they need to decide for themselves." That can be valid to some extent, especially with a new technology, but just as often it's a copout. There comes a time when leadership must insist on a direction. Most people want to believe that it'll be appropriate and appreciated for them to support a new technology. Leadership can't be ambivalent about that. If they are, they should spend their time and money on something they can support.

An important reason for having both a Steering Team and certification is to help deal with employee turnover. If you're implementing something that you expect to continue for more than a few months, you will have people—occasionally key people— changing jobs. If the ownership of the implementation or the tools is concentrated with a small number of people, your implementation will be at risk when they leave. Protect your company—build ownership as widely as possible.

EXAMPLE

I once interviewed a director of new product development in an engineer-to-order company. He was using our software very successfully, having significantly increased speed and reliability and improved the trust between development and manufacturing. When I asked, "Will it continue when you leave?" he replied, "Yes." Two years later he left. Within a year after that, critical chain scheduling was gone. He had failed to institutionalize his processes.

Communication

Ongoing communication is a critically important part of PPM, in several ways.

It's very rare that you can implement a major change everywhere at once. You might plan more and more projects using the critical chain approach, but doing them all at once in any but the smallest organizations would require an army of consultants. At any given time, you have people who understand a lot about the new approach, people who understand a little, and people who understand nothing. These people are constantly communicating with one another, which is why rumors (good and bad) start to fly once an implementation gets under way. Positive rumors can get people ready to adopt a new technology before you're ready to give it to them; negative rumors can get them ready to resist.

This incremental nature of an implementation implies a need for *marketing*, which I defined in Chapter 15 as "getting people to feel a particular way about something." You want people to feel comfortable with the idea of a PPM implementation, without them necessarily having to understand exactly what it is. If you don't tell them what's going on, they will figure it out themselves;

whether correctly or incorrectly. For those who understand nothing or a little, we want to make sure they aren't getting the wrong message or communicating the wrong message to others. We also want people to start to feel comfortable with the new language. Marketing—using presentations, webinars, web site, newsletters, and so on—needs to be done.

A good PPM marketing message might talk about the urgency to change, the vision for change, and how and when the changes are going to affect the organization. It may use some of the new language. It won't go into the details of how the change will occur. You want people to understand "how" only when they're ready to use that knowledge. Otherwise, when you're ready to teach them, they will already think they understand.

Ongoing feedback of status and results to the organization is also important. Not only does this provide a positive marketing message, but—as we saw in Chapter 15—it also validates expectations that have been set, improving trust and credibility.

These kinds of communication elements imply a need for a PPM Communication Plan. This is a plan, usually maintained by the PMO, that tracks who is communicating what to whom. It includes marketing, feedback, Steering Team meetings, and so on. It helps to communicate vision, urgency, and value associated with the implementation.

One element of the Communication Plan may be *branding*. Many of our clients brand PPM with their own name or terminology, increasing ownership in PPM by the organization.

Training

Training provides the groundwork for experiential learning. Training should be done as closely as possible to the activities people are being trained for, because the kinds of skills needed for

PPM expertise must be learned through hands-on experience as well as classroom training.[7]

A set of PowerPoint slides and a lecture are not sufficient to learn a new language or to learn PPM (or critical chain scheduling). We often see organizations whose "implementation plan" for a new technology such as software consists primarily of training people. When the time comes to apply their new knowledge, people are not able to do it effectively.

Certification and mentoring are important. Training can also be augmented by team meetings. Project teams meet regularly to talk about project status, impact chains, and so on. Functional organizations should meet regularly to talk about work rules, behavior changes, and inefficiencies.

Exercise

1. Analyze the mechanisms your organization has to institutionalize its processes. Which of those mechanisms would you need to change in order to institutionalize critical chain scheduling?

PART

ACHIEVING THE VISION

Before PPM, Imventure was driven by milestones. PPM required them to change from milestones to working as quickly as possible, from *train schedules* to *relay races*. This affected not just how people tracked and reported their work, but how they thought and talked about it.

In order to manage uncertainty, Imventure employees learned to schedule their projects by taking protection time out of individual task duration estimates, instead estimating task durations based on "focused" times. Some of the protection that was removed from tasks was pooled into "buffers." Buffer consumption was also used to report the status of projects; for example, projects with a lot of work and little buffer remaining were in serious trouble. The PPM implementation process had to embed the concepts of *buffers* and *buffer management* in Imventure's culture.

Switching to the relay race and using focused durations required basic changes to how people performed their day-to-day work. For those changes to take hold, Imventure had to create, teach, and adapt explicit *work rules* to help people stay on task.

Melding these changes into a synchronized whole required first of all that Imventure have a vision for its implementation. This is at the core of the very first PPM principle, "Ownership." Imventure's implementation vision statement was, "In order to fulfill our mission of saving and improving the lives of people around the world, we will become the best in our industry at building a solid, predictable product pipeline and bringing safe and effective medicines to market quickly and efficiently."

Let's assume we have this kind of vision, which includes emphasis on speed and predictability. Let's also assume that we understand the basic principles discussed in Part 1 and that we have the tools, behaviors and processes described in Part 2. How do we combine these pieces to achieve the vision? How do we keep people from deciding that we are just engaged in more Duck Farming?

The first and biggest challenge to achieving the vision is to build ownership in that vision. People have to want it enough to take responsibility for making it happen. They have to feel the urgency of desire to change. One reason that's difficult is past experience: in many companies, people have experienced time and again the failed improvement processes, the painful software systems, the broken promises.

The pilot process, described in Chapter 17, is essentially a foray into an implementation. The pilot is where the vision starts to meet the organization. A pilot builds understanding of both the effects of the past and what's likely to happen in the future, including who might and might not feel an urgency to change. By seeing how the pilot process worked at Imventure, you'll glimpse some important aspects of a real-life pilot.

Urgency drives vision, and everyone's sense of urgency is going to be different. Many authors on change management talk about urgency as if it's something that is shared across the organization.

That can only be true of the smallest organizations. In reality, senior executives worry about their message to Wall Street or the Board; technicians worry about their job review; Ph.D. scientists worry about their ability to get their research funded. These are some external concerns that drive them. And yet, if these people aren't pulling in the same direction, an implementation will lose steam. The organization may get some short-term results, but they're seldom sustainable. To synchronize an implementation, we not only need to connect the implementation and its vision to the company's goals; everyone's personal sense of urgency must also be tied to the implementation, *and people must understand that connection.*

Communication is critically important. It's not enough to do the work; you have to set expectations beforehand, and validate afterward that they came to pass or discuss why they weren't met (see also Chapter 15). As we examine the rollout process at Imventure, Chapter 18 discusses planning and organizing. You might notice that communication is at the heart of all of that. Without planning, information will still flow—but in ways you don't expect. We conclude in Chapter 19 with a discussion of how Imventure will continue to employ PPM to get more of the promised billions in benefits.

THE PPM PILOT

Why Pilot?

A PPM implementation usually starts with a pilot, a small implementation for a small number of projects. A pilot consists normally of a few Project Launches, although sometimes it makes sense to include multi-project tools and analysis.

A pilot's purpose is to gain understanding of what is likely to happen if or when PPM is implemented company-wide. This understanding will help company management and external or internal consultants decide whether and (if appropriate) how to spread the implementation across the organization. It will provide a "jumping-off point" for future improvements. Many areas of understanding are important, for example:

- Benefits and leverage (e.g. speed, predictability, productivity)
- Obstacles and risks (technical, cultural, attitudes and level of urgency of individual people or groups, current measurements, organizational structure)
- Costs (personnel, consulting, software, time)

People sometimes presume that the purpose of a pilot is to get some quick benefits and "prove" that the PPM approach works well, so that consultants can sell their products. That is actually a small part of the equation. After all, by using the examples of the Confetti Factory and appropriate reference stories, we can quickly demonstrate that PPM makes sense and could produce tremendous benefits. The pilot provides very important information that helps us to understand the obstacles and pressures that project teams in a specific organization are likely to face in adopting PPM principles. Table 4 shows some of the kinds of pressures against change on the left, with the kinds of replacements we'll need to plan for with the rollout on the right.

Some people object to the idea of piloting a critical chain implementation. The two most common objections are that you won't

TABLE 4	Project team pressures
PRESSURE AGAINST CHANGE	**PRESSURE FOR CHANGE**
Nothing in the way I'm measured would compel me to change.	I understand the global reasons for change, and how I will be affected if I don't change.
No one else is doing it.	Everyone is talking about how well the pilot went.
I don't have time to do it.	I see a clear benefit to investing the needed time.
I don't want people looking too closely at what I'm doing, because I'm not sure they'll like what they see.	Management no longer tolerates hidden problems, but is willing to help people solve them.
Our culture won't let me set and keep priorities.	I have clear, stable priorities; the effects of my not following those priorities are visible to everyone.
I don't understand why I should change.	The benefits of change are clear to everyone.

see the impact of implementing across the organization, and that the pilot implementation may not last because you're not changing enough of the organization. These observations are often correct, but they miss the true point of the pilot.

You can get big benefits quickly from PPM without proving that the benefits can be repeated more broadly. In fact, there will be no proof until you do it. However, preparation is important. The pilot helps you to understand why the benefits were achieved, what obstacles are likely to be encountered in the rollout, and what the likely costs will be. With this understanding, the impact of implementing more broadly must then be assessed soberly and a rollout plan developed. The PPM pilot isn't just a test of the methodology; it's an analysis of the organization.[1]

The pilot will almost certainly produce short-term benefits. Longer-term benefits are less certain, which is why a pilot is intended to evaluate a rollout of PPM, rather than just to get one-time benefits on a couple of projects. In order to understand why a pilot can't be a long-term solution, it's important to understand where this uncertainty of longer-term benefits comes from.

PPM is ultimately a synchronization process, helping people to work together more effectively. People who are not included in the pilot may not understand what you're trying to accomplish. Uninvolved projects, resource groups, or senior managers may inadvertently interfere with the pilot. Over the long run, the friction created when a few people are doing something new while the rest aren't will likely reduce the benefits. What we typically find in piloting a Project Launch is that project managers continue using the schedules. Without a broader implementation, however, standard dysfunctional behaviors (including multitasking) gradually come back to the project teams as the default organizational culture reasserts its grip.

EXAMPLE

In 2000, a division of a Global 100 company did a Project Launch with us, then a couple more. From their perspective, the primary purpose of these launches was short-term benefits rather than incorporating the PPM concepts into the way they do business. The launches were very successful for this. After a year, they decided to conduct further launches themselves, still without a real commitment to change. They had some success for about a year, but as new people came on board they skipped some important steps and results declined. Some years later, the company publicly declared the implementation to be a failure, even though there was no real implementation, and in fact the projects we were involved with were phenomenally successful. We learned our lesson; nowadays we rarely do multiple follow-on pilots.

Most people in larger organizations have no question about whether or not a pilot is a good idea. Jumping with both feet blindly into a major change effort is high risk, no matter how good the process looks to be. If you're making important changes to an organization, it's your responsibility to find out as much as possible before trying to make those changes. Here are four rules for parachuting into a new location: (1) understand the terrain before you leave the plane; (2) open the chute; (3) keep your feet together during landing; and (4) avoid any remaining quicksand and alligators you missed when following rule (1). Rule 1 is crucial.

Tip

A pilot in a company often produces many requests from others in the company who want to try PPM or the critical chain approach with their project or business unit. These requests are one measure of people's urgency to change. They are good, but you need to think through a good means for handling them. "Go do it yourself" is not normally a good means, because failures of people doing it themselves will become obstacles to the implementation.

The Pilot Process

Here are a few of the key elements of the PPM pilot process:

Learning: Before you start training people or installing software, learn as much as you can about the organization. What is the management structure? What is the culture of the organization? What obstacles might you expect to encounter? While the pilot process will generate much more knowledge, it's always wise to study the landscape before you leave the plane. One way to do this is through interviews.

Steering Team: Charter a Steering Team of the most senior-level people who can be involved. They should be the ones to decide whether a rollout makes sense. The team should include a sponsor who "owns" the PPM pilot. The team will have to be trained, they will need to be given regular updates on the pilot's status, and you will need to learn their concerns. If you can't put together a senior-level Steering Team, your chances of a successful long-lasting rollout of PPM are significantly reduced. There's a good chance you'll have to do a second pilot to bring a Steering Team on board.

We discussed the functions of the Steering Team in Chapter 16. Their major job is to communicate the importance of the implementation, so that it will be taken seriously. For a pilot, the Steering Team must also evaluate how well the pilot is working, and what would be required to expand PPM to the entire organization.

Message: Determine the problems the organization is trying to solve and the urgency with which the people need to solve it. Help the Steering Team create a simple vision statement that will be used to communicate this. The Steering Team must own that vision, because they must promote it.

Implementation plan: As always, planning is important. You'll need to keep track of what's going on, you'll need to report status (especially to the Steering Team), and you'll want to demonstrate how PPM applies to implementation projects as well as others. Regular implementation project updates are a great way to manage Steering Team expectations and expose people quickly to the PPM vocabulary.

Individual project scheduling: A big part of a pilot is to work with project teams to help them schedule individual projects. That scheduling process normally results in valuable insights and changed behaviors that can produce very positive results. It also results in success stories that can be used to describe the reasons for doing a rollout.

Multi-project pilot work: Sometimes it makes sense to put the project schedules together and analyze them using the multi-project capabilities in ProChain Enterprise. This activity requires training and assessment. Additional interviews may be required in order to assess the resource picture.

Project team follow-up: The new PPM behaviors don't become habits overnight. Facilitators may need to sit in on project team meetings for several weeks after they go live with the schedule. That's the way to make sure the right thinking, communication, and data collection are taking place.

Regular Steering Team meetings: Throughout the implementation the Steering Team should be kept apprised of the pilot's status. You will want to talk with them frequently in order to understand, from team member perspectives, what is and isn't working.

Assess and Transfer: After all the projects have been scheduled and results data collected, we usually schedule an assessment presentation with the Steering Team in order to present our findings, conclusions, and recommendations.

Assessing the Pilot

We should understand a few things as we assess a pilot:

What is the present urgency to change? This question is fundamental. Without urgency, nothing will change. Keep in mind that the concept of urgency is not organizational, but individual. Level and type of urgency may be different for different individuals, functions, projects, and business units.

Keep in mind that often, when people discuss urgency to do something, they're talking about someone else's urgency and don't realize it. An executive in charge of project management for a large corporation once told me, "It's important to me to do well on these projects. But it's even more important for my boss." Translated, that meant he perceived urgency, but it wasn't *his* urgency.

What will be the obstacles and risks to adopting the PPM principles? It's hard to plan for a trip if you don't know how far you have to go. Very often, during a pilot, people will try to "adapt" PPM so they can manage projects the way they've always done it. Sometimes management is unwilling to put time into supporting the change process. These kinds of lessons give a useful picture of what might happen in a full implementation.

What existing policies and processes will affect a rollout? The more obstacles that are left in place, the more difficult the rollout will be. On the other hand, the more things have to change, the more people will be nervous about changing. It's valuable to prioritize obstacles and risks. Typically a very few need to be addressed immediately and others will need to be addressed over the course of a rollout.

What are the potential benefits of PPM? The pilot should give a good idea of the kinds of benefits that are possible: time saved during planning and execution, schedule reliability, employee satisfaction, etc. These benefits are obviously approximate; if you wait until the pilot projects have been completed before assessing likely benefits, you will potentially wait a year or two. A common objection when using pilot data to describe benefits is, "We could have done this anyway" or "We did this, but it's not something that could be done often." Those comments may or may not be true, but they miss the point: the potential for benefits, in any number of areas, should help inform a decision for a broader implementation.

What would the rollout look like? This includes both a preliminary plan, and estimates of the associated costs and risks.

Piloting at Imventure

Imventure chose to pilot PPM on two different new products. One pilot was for a "Phase 2" clinical trial for a smaller group of patients, in which the company would learn about the efficacy and risks associated with the drug. This would be scheduled up to its next big decision point, namely, whether or not to proceed with Phase 3 trials. The second project was for a "Phase 3" trial, to confirm efficacy with a much larger number of patients and to evaluate longer-term safety. These projects were both key studies for important products, and management decided that they would enable the necessary learning about PPM.

To start, a senior management Steering Team was set up. This team met monthly with the consultants in order to learn about PPM, monitor status, and ultimately evaluate the pilot. A sponsor was also identified who would help the consultants navigate

Imventure's culture. The sponsor and consultants together were called the "Implementation Team." The Implementation Team created an implementation plan, consisting not just of work needed to schedule individual projects but also of various critical planning, assessment, and Steering Team activities.

One of the critical planning elements was a PPM Communication Plan, essentially a map of the communication activities that needed to take place with different groups. The communication plan helped to communicate the vision, urgency, and value of the implementation. The vision statement created by the Implementation Team was mentioned at the start of part 3: "In order to fulfill our mission of saving and improving the lives of people around the world, we will become the best in our industry at building a solid, predictable product pipeline and bringing safe and effective medicines to market quickly and efficiently." Specific communication activities were tailored to the sense of urgency and value of specific groups. For example, a PPM overview presentation to Regulatory Affairs might emphasize the importance of safe and effective medicines; a presentation to Marketing might emphasize speed and predictability.

The process for each project team was similar. The Implementation Team assigned a consultant to work with each team. The consultants interviewed team members and did the preparatory work for the project planning, including helping to form Network Build Teams for the pilots. They met with the project team members to train them on the concepts and principles of PPM. After the project plan was created, the consultants stayed on to help during the updating process to make sure the team continued to work proactively to find ways to speed up the project. They also collected assessment information—anecdotes, concrete actions associated with benefits and risks, surveys, obstacles, and so on—in preparation for a written assessment of each PPM Project Launch. This entire process, from interviews through assessment, took about three months of elapsed time for each project, with five or six days of time required from each Network Build Team. Overall, the piloting process took four months.

The Implementation Team collected data to evaluate some likely key resources for later multi-project planning. Detailed analysis, training, and deployment were saved for later.

The Implementation Team collected a great deal of useful information through the pilot effort, and summarized it in an assessment presentation to the Steering Team. That assessment had to answer the following questions:

What is the present urgency to change?

At the senior management level, there was a great deal of urgency to change. This urgency was described in part 1. However, as it percolated down through the layers of the organization, from Vice-Presidents to Directors to functional and project managers to individual contributors, this urgency quickly translated from "Our projects must become faster and more predictable" to "We must accept more and more work while continuing to hit our milestones." At the top, this pressure was perceived as urgency to change; at the bottom, it was perceived as pressure to work harder, not smarter. This would clearly be a big element to address during the rollout.

What will be the obstacles and risks to adopting the PPM principles?

The difficulties Imventure had with the PPM principles were described in Chapter 8. The overall problem was that the milestone system caused various behaviors that appeared more and more dysfunctional as the organization became increasingly stressed. This grew especially clear during the pilots, as some people tried to behave according to their milestone world while using the PPM schedules. Here are some symptoms of that:

- For one pilot, people worked hard to make sure that no tasks were late and no buffers were consumed. Analysis confirmed that people were treating the task durations as milestones and counting down their durations to a due date, rather than thinking through the work remaining and the focused time the work should take.
- The other project team was initially unwilling to meet and update the project plan. While they recognized significant benefits during the network building process, they were not accustomed to regular updates and team meetings. It wasn't until a sit-down discussion with the team, going through the pros and cons, that they agreed to continue using the schedule.
- Some managers continued asking for dates, even though they were being given regular buffer information. This had to be dealt with on a case-by-case basis to train and mentor the responsible individuals.

What existing policies and processes will affect a rollout?

The milestone policies drove most of Imventure's processes. For example:

- Individuals were expected to hit milestones, rather than speed projects to completion with minimal multitasking.
- Computer systems were designed for milestone reporting. Buffers and buffer consumption would not fit into existing reports.
- Imventure negotiated milestones with its vendors, then put in place penalties if they missed them. They would have been better off negotiating a process whereby vendors made more money if they were able to speed up the important work.
- Portfolio-level project priorities were quickly converted to milestones as they were absorbed into the organization. As

discussed earlier, milestones are not priorities. The need in a rollout would not be just to set priorities, but also to find means of communicating them.

What are the potential benefits of PPM?

Or, in other words, "Could a PPM rollout achieve the vision we have expressed?" The projects were each about a year away from completion. Over the four months of the pilot, each of the projects documented between four and six weeks of likely project acceleration from actions that the teams agreed would probably not otherwise have been taken. Furthermore, because of the use of buffers, all team members and senior management felt that predictability, including the chances of hitting the pre-existing commitment dates, was dramatically increased. Surveys of project team members indicated that they were completing projects substantially more quickly and reliably.

One project, if successful, was anticipated to be worth two hundred million dollars a year; the other five hundred million per year. Even factoring this by the very real probability that any given compound might have bad results from its trials, and therefore not make it to market, the value of the pilot to Imventure was many millions of dollars, achieved in just a few months. Depending on how the results would scale, even assuming that only a fraction of the projects survived to produce a marketable product, application on thirty similar projects over two years could easily get Imventure to a billion dollars in real impact.

While these benefits are indicative of what could be done, there was no guarantee that—should Imventure have decided *not* to implement PPM more broadly—similar benefits would continue to be realized for the projects in the pilot. That's because interference from the rest of the organization—difficulties setting priorities, interruptions and requests for multitasking, staffing changes, and so on—could ultimately have resulted in the pilot momentum being lost, and, eventually, the PPM effort dying out. People would not move backwards relative to the documented benefits, but various milestone-driven behaviors such as multitasking and inadequate planning would reassert themselves.

What would a rollout look like?

It was clear there were several initiatives that Imventure would need to pursue in order to make the rollout successful. The most critical would be the transition from milestones to having clear project and task priorities. This would require real top-down planning for the implementation so as to minimize confusion and make sure the coexistence of old and new behaviors, always present at some point during a change process, would do no damage.

As you might have guessed, as a result of the pilot Imventure decided to move ahead with a full implementation of PPM. A description of their rollout effort is given in the following chapters.

Exercises

1. Think of a way you might measure the value of a PPM rollout in dollars per day. How would you set up a pilot in your organization to collect the necessary data? You might, for example, try to estimate the potential overall improvement in project-related revenues; you might factor in the potential for increased market share. Substantial product development costs can be saved through better planning, but there's a good chance the potential for cost savings will be dwarfed by the potential for additional revenue.[2]
2. Review (in table 4) the pressures against change. Which seem like valid reasons, and which seem like excuses? What do you think the underlying reasons behind the excuses might be?

PLANNING AND
ORGANIZING THE ROLLOUT

For Imventure's rollout of PPM, we will look mainly at its first year. That's the time with the most changes, the greatest potential for benefits, and the greatest risks. As a fictional example, it will be simplified compared with any real case study. While the kinds of issues and approaches described here are typical of any organization that develops new products, they are not by any means exhaustive.

Due to their pilot experiences, Imventure's Steering Team recognized from the start that there was going to be a major problem to address, beyond any technical PPM implementation planning: language. Because of the milestone culture at Imventure, people did not have a vocabulary that allowed them to meaningfully talk about uncertainty or priorities in a relay race world. The switch in PPM to pooling uncertainty into buffers requires pulling padding out of tasks; this would be a big change in how people reported their status and how they would be measured on the status they reported.

The switch from milestones to priorities requires even more than reporting and measurements; it means a mindset switch from priorities being "what, from everything I could work on, will most help me make my commitments" to "what, from everything I could work on, will most help us complete our projects quickly and reliably." Instead of milestone commitments they would have duration estimates. The differences for Imventure and its people were profound.

Simply training people in the new concepts and expecting them to change how they worked would be like showing people martial arts movies and expecting them to be effective in combat. The language problem was complicated by the fact that a PPM implementation cannot be done with the flip of a switch. It takes time to learn the language and to create and use meaningful PPM schedules. Therefore, total immersion in the new language was not feasible. PPM thinking would have to coexist with milestone thinking.

The Steering Team wanted to address the language problem by breaking it into two parts: dealing with the internal issues, especially milestones, and dealing with vendors. After reviewing some pieces of the basic implementation planning, we'll see an overview of their approach.

Basic Implementation Planning

Many of the key PPM rollout planning elements are similar to those we've discussed for the pilot: forming a Steering Team, creating a message, and so on. These pieces were included in a critical chain project plan, along with some additional pieces needed for the full rollout.

The Steering Team's responsibilities changed in some subtle ways. After deciding to implement PPM, they needed to take more ownership in making it happen. This required a firm public commitment from all Steering Team members. It also required that any apparent obstacles needed to be brought up and dealt with quickly by Steering Team members; waiting around for next month's meeting, or for a problem to solve itself, was unacceptable.

In the pilot, the Implementation Team (consisting mainly of consultants) operated behind the scenes. For the rollout, the

Implementation Team was owned by Imventure. The Implementation Team had people in several roles:

- Consultants: In real life, these can be external or internal, depending on whether the organization has PPM expertise available. Imventure used external consultants.
- Lead Consultant: This is the consultant responsible for managing the implementation from the point of view of the consulting organization.
- Director of the Project Management Office (PMO): The PMO head at Imventure reported to the VP of Development.
- Certification Candidates: Imventure selected seven people to be trained and certified by the consultants in PPM processes. These people were part of the PMO. They were to be equipped both to facilitate the PPM launch process and to train other certified PPM Experts.

The vision, which included speed and predictability as critical components, continued from the pilot. The PPM Communication Plan was expanded to encompass the entire drug development organization. Since gears had shifted from "shall we do this" to "we're doing this," many more marketing and communication activities were planned.

The Implementation Team decided to re-brand PPM as "Project Velocity" in order to increase the feeling of ownership and provide a greater sense that "this is how we do business."

Initial training was also planned. There were some new Steering Team members to be trained and training was also needed for the Implementation Team. The Process Review Board (see below) also had to be brought up to speed.

The IT department was brought in to help expand the deployment of the ProChain Enterprise software. While the installation for the pilot was very limited and therefore didn't require major IT controls and review, the rollout was a different matter. IT could become a limiting factor if it did not begin early.

There were early discussions about how to standardize resource types, to allow cross-project resource analysis to be done as schedules were created. While it was important to start this standardization early, Imventure recognized that it would be several months before they gathered sufficient data to start examining interesting resource capacity and loading questions.

Milestone Behaviors

We've already discussed Imventure's milestone culture. The basic issues for the rollout can be summarized as follows.

- Language: There were ingrained patterns of thinking, behaving, and most of all communicating.
- Dual systems: People would have to operate in relay race and milestone worlds at the same time.
- Measurements: Management had to switch both formal and informal reward systems to change the meaning of "sin" from that of the milestone world to the relay race world. The sin was no longer to miss a milestone; it was to drop the baton. Of course, being ready for the baton—switching from the train schedule to the relay race approach—requires good planning and communication on the part of both the passer and the receiver. Usually this requires a significant change in attitude.

Process Review Board

Early on, Imventure created what they called a Process Review Board (PRB). This group reported directly to the head of drug development, and consisted of well-respected Director-level individuals from key functions across the product development organization. The PRB's overall charter was to ensure that the move from milestones to relay races happened as smoothly a possible. That meant obstacles had to be anticipated and problems dealt with quickly. The PRB had several important functions.

The first function was to map out the kinds of changes that would be necessary. For example, they knew that many people would be torn between the old way of working and the new way. Therefore they needed some overall work rules, approved at a high level, that would help people with tasks in both critical chain and milestone projects. They came up with the following sequencing rules for deciding in what order to work tasks.

- When you are deciding between tasks from milestone schedules, decide as you always have.
- When you are deciding between tasks from critical chain and milestone schedules, work tasks according to the project sequence determined by the PRB.
- When you are deciding between tasks in critical chain projects, prioritize by projected time and percent task impact (PTI). Note that this rule may at times encourage people to work on projects that are clearly inferior in terms of value to the company. They decided to start with this rule, and revise it if conflicts became apparent.

One important change that needed to be mapped out had to do with adapting IT systems. Imventure had a number of computerized systems to track and report milestones. Eventually their function would be taken over by ProChain Enterprise (PCE) or adjusted to support revised reporting needs. The PRB recognized that the old systems, while promoting the old vocabulary and ways of working, could not go away for some time. Therefore they chartered a team, including members of the PRB, PMO, and IT, to create a plan to both integrate the new Project Velocity information into executive dashboards and to phase out the old milestone systems where and when appropriate.

Their second function was to come up with processes for sequencing projects, and for communicating that sequencing throughout the organization. These processes would then need to be approved by the Steering Team. An initial problem with doing this was that they started their work with the word "prioritize," which has win-lose connotations. If one thing is given a higher priority, another will have a lower. Eventually, they came to the conclusion that the word "prioritize," while correct, is too loaded with extra meanings. They settled on "sequence." It's a reasonable compromise, in the sense that while Imventure management wanted to finish all the projects that had been approved, they knew that trying to work on them all at the same time didn't make sense.

The third PRB function was to examine and change milestone measurements for critical chain projects. Because people are supposed to be estimating focused durations and might take more or less time than estimated, you don't want to punish them for being late. Essentially, the PRB decided that people's schedule performance should be measured based on adherence to the work rules. That included not only the sequencing rules, but other work rules as well. For example, chronic multitasking would be considered equivalent to missing milestones. Naturally, this process would have to go hand-in-hand with training so that new expectations were well understood.

A related decision was to start getting people to view milestone dates as forecasts rather than commitments. That would allow people to continue to look at and talk about dates, but also allow them the possibility of missing the dates or of finishing work early. That was a great way to change milestone behaviors without having to eliminate the milestones entirely.

The final PRB function was to provide ongoing oversight and review. Members were actively engaged in checking to make sure that the new processes (work rules, project sequencing, measurements, and so on) were working. They were making sure that personnel changes, especially management changes, wouldn't cause problems due to lack of understanding or buy-in. They were also constantly reviewing and addressing questions and complaints from people at all levels of the organization. Leads of Project Velocity projects in particular were encouraged to report problems and assured that problems would be dealt with in a positive way. Small problems had to be dealt with quickly, before they became big. People tend to be skeptical of management's willingness to change and they don't have to be burned many times to be persuaded to avoid the fire.

Sometimes people were uncomfortable giving focused duration estimates for their tasks, occasionally to the point of refusing to provide input. This had to be dealt with by the PRB as quickly as possible, on a function-by-function basis. Occasionally, the wrong person was on the team. More commonly, people were afraid of making commitments that their group would not support.

The answer was not just to get approval from the group; it was to take the opportunity to explain, again and again, that task estimates are only "best guesses," and if an estimate were off (which it usually will be) the buffers would help protect the project. If the person needed help to come up with an estimate, they got it; if they needed approval, that was considered to be an opportunity for more learning.

The Steering Team could have begun certification and the PPM Launches before completing any of their work. However, in order not to have to retrain project teams on revised work rules, they decided to get the work rules and project sequencing process going before beginning the launches. They recognized that these activities would be on the impact chain for the implementation and were able to get them going quickly. Fortunately, the last two PRB functions, measurements and review, could happen in parallel with the Launches and other implementation work.

In the end, the most difficult problem that the PRB had to deal with was management itself. Management's autocratic "Duck Farming" approach to setting deadlines, both a byproduct and enabler of milestone management, was difficult to tackle. People were unwilling to report problems caused by their bosses, partly for fear of retaliation, partly because the Imventure culture considered such complaints to be unacceptable. And when people did report such problems, there was not always an effective mechanism for dealing with them, because some managers continued to believe that the autocratic style was the right style.

In most cases, continued reluctance to change was dealt with by messaging, mentoring, and measurements; occasionally people needed to be moved to more appropriate positions. Imventure wasn't able to fully solve its change problems until a couple of key people had been moved out of the company.

The second most difficult problem had to do with informal measurements. In the old system, while certain milestones were deemed "key" and tracked closely, others were not officially tracked or measured. However, in order to maintain some semblance of control, many managers tracked unofficial milestones and task due dates. That meant that just changing the formal measures was insufficient; informal tracking systems and measurements had to be unearthed and changed as well.

Implementation Activities

The Implementation Team worked closely with the PRB to incorporate work rules and processes into the Project Velocity training. They also made sure to add "marketing" activities into the Communication Plan. These were opportunities—existing and new—to spread the word about both the implementation vision and the new relay race approach. If you don't supply people with information about what's going on, they will make it up themselves and you may not be happy with the results. Imventure used many media to communicate the message, such as internal conferences, short presentations, brown-bag lunches, emails, newsletters, and more.

Vendor Management

The Steering Team realized that there was tremendous leverage in re-examining their relationships with vendors. Critical chain schedules could be created without vendor participation and their tasks treated as having no uncertainty. However, given Imventure's level of outsourcing, there was clearly much room for removing padding from vendor tasks and for speeding up projects.

To capitalize on the opportunity, a purchasing team was set up to learn about critical chain scheduling and to make recommendations for bringing some key vendors onboard. The purchasing team went to some critical chain training and sat in on a network building session. They made the following recommendations:

- Whenever possible, bring vendors into the project planning process. It's important for them to understand what the project teams are doing, and it's important for the project teams to better understand the vendors' work.
- Project Leads should incorporate the language of uncertainty and the importance of speed in their discussions with Purchasing about vendor contracting.
- Define contracting approaches that give vendors incentives to complete key tasks more quickly.
- Determine the types of tasks for which the new contracting approach would normally be preferred. It isn't sensible or even possible to change every relationship.
- Over the longer term, partner with vendors to bring them on board with critical chain and Project Velocity.

The contracting process turned out to be somewhat different for different vendors. It always started with some critical chain training. The basic elements for the "relay race contracts" were the same: penalties for being late, as had always been the case, along with rewards for being early, which would depend on the criticality of the work.

Imventure used many metrics to evaluate vendors, including quality and flexibility. For all its vendors, Imventure changed its schedule measure from a milestone approach to a speed approach. Earlier delivery was considered better, even in cases not associated with a monetary reward.

In the end, Imventure was able to accelerate key vendor tasks significantly, although usually at a cost. Besides that cost, there was a limit to what most vendors were willing to do; few were ready to fundamentally change how they did business. That's why, after the implementation's first year, Imventure started working on a partnering program to help vendors improve their project management. That way, Imventure could capitalize on the benefits experienced by its vendors.

Certification

Imventure went through the rigorous ProChain Expert Certification process for its seven certification candidates. This process consisted of ongoing mentoring by consultants, an acceptable level of understanding regarding various methodology components, and participation in several PPM Launches.

To help ensure that the process would proceed smoothly, the Implementation Team made sure that the candidates were full time employees, because certification of part-time people is difficult and slow. In addition, bi-weekly progress reports were emailed to the Steering Team, and monthly status was reported at Steering Team meetings, to help to make sure the PMO and certification candidates stayed focused on learning the Project Velocity methodology.

Exercises

1. Review this chapter from the point of view of whether the ground at Imventure is fertile for change. What was in place that would help ensure implementation success? What was missing?
2. Which is more important in a PPM rollout: the creation of new certified experts, or getting more projects using critical chain schedules?

LOOKING TO
THE FUTURE

Internal consultants should conduct a disciplined assessment of the status of their implementation on a regular basis. ProChain consultants conduct a formal assessment of a rollout when the Expert Certification process is finished. The assessment includes lessons learned and planning for next steps. It also includes a transfer process to help make sure that any remaining transfer of understanding, processes, or tools will be carried out. All this ensures that the ongoing relationship—including ongoing mentoring and evaluation—is clear.

Assessment and Lessons Learned

Imventure's implementation issues were first of all evaluated by referring back to the PPM principles. If an issue would have a negative effect on one or more principles, it needed serious discussion and evaluation. If not, chances were much greater that it wasn't important, or at least that it didn't need to be resolved immediately. Table 5 shows some of Imventure's achievements relative to the principles.

Bottom-line measurements were collected. During the first year of implementation, the projects scheduled averaged two months each of documented improvements in time to market. These data

TABLE 5	Imventure's achievements relative to the PPM principles
Ownership	Ongoing marketing efforts created widespread awareness. Planning and information feedback—to the Steering Team, project teams, and the organization as a whole—helped to create ownership. See the discussion of the Cycle of Results in Chapter 15.
Leverage	Imventure gained the ability to focus on real status and on what's important in projects. This produced direct, validated benefits for all concerned and helped point the way to future improvements.
Priorities	The prioritization or "sequencing" process, project schedules, and the PRB together created relatively clear priorities. However, getting those priorities adopted required ongoing work.
Status	The quality of status was a direct indicator of how well the changes were working, and it went up dramatically as more projects were scheduled. Duck Farming decreased but did not disappear.
Planning	The planning helped to deal with known problems; more importantly, it shined light into areas that previously couldn't be examined. That meant people could more effectively anticipate new obstacles and identify hitherto unknown organizational constraints.
Uncertainty	Over the course of the year, most people in the organization learned much about the language of uncertainty. This was greatly aided by the willingness of the Steering Team to speak this language themselves at every available opportunity.

justified the effort and expenses of the implementation many times over, and helped to ensure that the implementation would continue to be supported and funded by the Steering Team.

Human Resources

Imventure management learned during the pilot that more project management resources would be needed. Consider the right-hand box in figure 6.1, "People have little time for planning." This was the case at Imventure: little time was traditionally allocated to planning, meaning that little planning time was available for Project and Assistant Leads. Unfortunately, action wasn't taken until partway into the implementation, when feedback from numerous sources exposed the fact that sometimes Leads weren't able to spend needed time making sure their team was planning and executing properly. The Steering Team resolved to have one or two dedicated Leads for each project, depending on size. However, it wasn't possible to implement this immediately.

Similarly, there was a mismatch in responsibilities between Assistant Leads and Project Leads. For high-profile projects in particular, the Project Leads tended to be fairly high-level people. While they had the authority to make day-to-day decisions for the project, they didn't have the time and often didn't view it as their responsibility. The Assistant Lead, on the other hand, was a lower-level position without the authority to get things done. The immediate solution was to change slightly the definitions of Assistant Lead and Project Lead. Project Leads were still responsible for the outward-facing aspects of the project, but they were held more clearly responsible for project success, including meeting commitment dates. Assistant Leads were given more authority and responsibility over the day-to-day affairs of the project, assuming some responsibility for meeting project objectives and coming much closer to the standard definition of a project manager.[1] These changes allowed the Project Leads and the Assistant Leads more easily to drive the kind of focus that PPM enables.

Human Resources became involved in this process so as to improve the job definitions of Assistant Leads and Project Leads. They were also responsible for adding a job definition that included Project Velocity Experts, so that being certified would be viewed as a desirable thing. That ultimately led to the development of several levels of lead, with certification required in order to reach the highest levels.

Existing Initiatives

Some existing initiatives caused friction during the implementation. In general, these were easily managed. In one case, the implementation of project time management using Imventure's Enterprise Resource Planning system, the Steering Team had to intervene and halt the time management project. In another case, the Steering Team concluded that additional expertise in process improvement technologies would be helpful to the implementation. They therefore placed a Six Sigma expert on the PRB.

Imventure managers learned to be more careful with their questions and to consider carefully how they would be perceived. In one case, a team worked hard and successfully to accelerate a project, to the extent that they could commit to finishing it a month earlier than expected. The business unit that owned the project came back to the team with the question, "Can you accelerate it another month?" The team felt that, despite having worked hard and effectively, their efforts weren't appreciated.

The management question was valid, although a better expression might have been, "That's great! Is there any way we can help to bring this in another month earlier?" One valid team response might have been, "No, and here's why." Another might have been, "Here are some things we can try, here are the likely costs and here are the likely time savings." Instead, the team felt as though they were back to being pressured to say "yes" to an impossible task.

Transfer

A number of ongoing efforts were begun by the consultants and then taken over by the PMO. During the Expert Certification process, the PMO head took over ownership of the certification plan. In addition, the PMO managed the induction and training of all certification candidates after the first five. Ongoing reports of implementation status (including new certification candidates, projects scheduled, results achieved, etc.) became part of the standard PMO reporting process.

The PMO head appointed one of the Project Velocity Experts to be in charge of materials and processes. That process owner was responsible for training materials, documentation, standard implementation plans, and so on. He was also responsible for collecting suggested methodology changes, which would be reviewed by all the Project Velocity Experts before inclusion in the standard materials. And finally, the process owner had to coordinate any software updates that would affect the implementation.

As the implementation progressed, the consultants phased out their involvement with the PRB, leaving that responsibility to the PMO head. The consultants did continue to check status reports from the PMO in order to bring an extra set of experienced eyes to their activities. In addition, the consultants were brought in a few times each year to check on the status of new Experts: Did they have a deep knowledge of the tools and processes? Was Imventure continuing to certify individuals who were qualified to do what was needed?

Next Steps

Changes to Imventure's Human Resources processes were slow and difficult. HR procedures, in particular job descriptions, are often intentionally difficult to change. If they change too quickly, without adequate review and communication, serious confusion can result. Here is a summary of the kinds of changes that continued after the first year of implementation:

- The job description for Assistant Leads was expanded to include multiple job titles, in order adequately to represent different levels of qualifications.

- Measurements, for Assistant Leads and others, needed review and change. Ideas like "ability to multitask" and "accommodating project needs expressed by management" were replaced by ideas like "focus" and "project success."
- While the PRB's IT team was able to change dashboards and reports, some of the old milestone systems continued into the second year. When all significant projects were scheduled through Project Velocity, it was time to shut down some old systems. This was also the job of the IT team working closely with the PMO.

Many of the year-two changes relate back to the idea that the definition of "good" performance may need to change with PPM, to take on a more global perspective. Good task performance is certainly good, good project performance is better, and good portfolio performance is better still. Good company performance is best of all. The more globally oriented people's measurements, the better for the company.

As more and more schedules were up and running with PPM, Imventure gradually moved to doing analysis based on project resource requirements. They were able to analyze and plan based on better project and resource information. They could better and better integrate their historical knowledge of potential project benefits and risks with new-found understanding of timing, cost, and capacity. During the first year, work was begun in the following areas, with the intention of pursuing ongoing improvements:

- A standard templating process for different types of projects. Selecting and refining a template became part of the project approval process. That helped significantly in estimating timing and moving down the path toward better resource management.

- Addressing direct leverage points for the organization. This included starting projects based on available capacity (i.e. project pacing), but also went further to address the next logical question: Given the projects we need to complete, what resources do we need? This effort required good templates and a disciplined process for starting, managing, and terminating projects.
- Portfolio analysis and planning, based on project timing and resource requirements.
- Vendor partnerships so that vendors would adopt Project Velocity techniques.[2]

Tip

Some companies seem unable to kill old projects, even as newer projects with much higher impact are begun. This results in a huge backlog, and often management loses track of what projects are active. The new-old problem is typically "solved" by creating a two-level system: the "top ten" (or "top twenty," "super projects," "red list," or something similar) on one level, and everything else on the other. Everything on the first-level list is higher priority; everything else is lower. This usually ends up as a way of addressing the problem without solving it, because management still wants everything they know about to be done as quickly as possible. How much attention should be paid to off-list projects? How much is enough for the top projects? The tough decisions still haven't been made.

It's important to decide what to do. It's just as important to decide what not to do.

AFTERWORD

I t's fitting now to revisit briefly the title of this book, *The Billion Dollar Solution*, and think about where the billions of dollars come from. How do we get to the Billion Dollar Picture described in the Introduction? For a moment, imagine what it would be like to inhabit a world in which . . .

. . . people work on their tasks from start to finish, with minimal interruptions: **single-tasking**. Stress from the Multitasking Maelstrom is gone. The need for speed is as strong as ever, but the need to juggle five bowling balls is gone. Productivity is way up, comparable to the 30 percent in the confetti factory. Project cycle times are down dramatically, anywhere from 20 percent to 50 percent. Variability in task and project durations is dramatically reduced.

. . . task and project commitments are realistic, based on our best information: **no more Duck Farming**. Variability is acknowledged. We have realistic status information; we know which decisions need to be made and we can make those decisions based on good information. Stress is down, trust is up.

. . . the highest priority tasks on the highest priority projects are known, and are worked in that priority sequence: the **relay race**. Not only do we know where the leverage points are for our projects, but we focus on those areas. By knowing what's more important, we also know what's less important and don't have to spend extraordinary effort on those things. We use our improved productivity, speed, and predictability as competitive advantages.

. . . we have sufficient trust that our people are being used effectively and that we can purchase and apply resources based on real needs: **resource management**. Rather than negotiating for what people think they might need in the midst of the maelstrom, we have sufficient order and sufficient credible data to make well-reasoned resourcing decisions. We improve data quality on an ongoing basis by managing the tradeoff between effort and data value. Our staff is highly productive and we are effectively staffed for speed and predictability.

This is a world not only of speed, predictability, and productivity but of order and clean air. Gone is the chaos, gone is the smoke of burning money. This is the world of the Billion Dollar Solution.

I have four final messages. First, there are phenomenal benefits that most organizations are *not* realizing today, benefits being left behind in such areas as speed, predictability, quality of life, and productivity. In a sense, these billions of dollars could be considered "hidden costs." This book helps point out where these costs are being incurred. They are present even in companies known for the effort they put into project management.

Second, while PPM can result in dramatic improvements, it is also a change process that takes time, resources, and expertise. Beware of those who say it doesn't; they are taking risks with *your* business. Here are some things you might hear:

- The cultural changes are not significant. (They are.)
- The primary means of bringing people up to speed is training. (Training is only one piece of the puzzle.)
- Keep your focus on the tools and features of the products you're being sold. (While these can be important, they must

be considered in the context of the overall methodology.)

- The implementation will be fast and simple. (This is sometimes true for very small organizations. It is occasionally true for small groups in larger organizations, depending on how independent they are. Lasting change is never fast and simple for large organizations.)

Third, for further information and content related to the ideas discussed in this book, see http://www.billiondollarsolution.com. And finally, seek out experienced help.

Exercises

1. Think through the value to your company of these and any other relevant aspects to the "PPM world." Compare that value to the value you expect from other improvement initiatives you are pursuing. Which should you be working on?
2. On the following page there is a quiz you can try. I hope your answers match mine.[1]

		PPM QUIZ
True	**False**	**Question**
☐	☐	1. The behavior changes needed to implement critical chain scheduling are minimal.
☐	☐	2. People can learn everything they need to know to implement the PPM methodology through books and training.
☐	☐	3. You must do detailed resource modeling in order to do valid critical chain scheduling.
☐	☐	4. It's important to get as many critical chain schedules in place as possible, as quickly as possible, in order to get everyone changed over to the new system as quickly as possible.
☐	☐	5. If you put in place the right tools, the behavior changes will happen by themselves.
☐	☐	6. An individual can have any number of highest-priority things to work on at any given time.
☐	☐	7. An organization can have any number of highest-priority projects at any given time.
☐	☐	8. Task durations should be commitments that you expect to keep.
☐	☐	9. You can't pilot PPM. As Yoda says, "Do or do not. There is no try."
☐	☐	10. There is nothing new in PPM or critical chain.
☐	☐	11. Critical chain scheduling is a silver bullet that will solve your project management problems.
☐	☐	12. The best workers are those adept at shifting their attention among many tasks with unclear priorities.
☐	☐	13. Project managers should expect to consume their entire project buffers by the time their project is completed.
☐	☐	14. If you pick a specific task to be highest priority, all of your other tasks will suffer.

APPENDIX A:
SUMMARY

ProChain Project Management (PPM) is a methodology that provides a significant return on investment, with relatively little risk to the organizations that implement it. The methodology has many pieces, which are summarized in this appendix.

RACER Hierarchy

The RACER diagram shows the different elements of PPM at a high level. At the bottom, we change behaviors, using the right tools and reshaped processes. This helps to activate the guiding principles. To realize the vision, it's necessary to activate the guiding principles. The vision usually includes improved speed, predictability, discipline, and/or productivity.

Realize the Vision

Activate the Guiding Principles

Change Behaviors
Employ the Right Tools
Reshape Processes

PPM Principles

The PPM principles form the theoretical basis for the PPM approach.

- Ownership
  Help everyone to understand and own the vision of the PPM implementation.
- Leverage
  Move as quickly as possible to complete work that is highly leveraged.
- Priorities
  Help each other to focus on the highest priorities and highest value. Strive to make them the same.
- Status
  Communicate real status across all levels of the organization, including passing on your work when "done."
- Planning
  Plan your work ahead of time in order to address problems when they're small.
- Uncertainty
  Uncertainty is part of reality. Account for it explicitly and minimize its impact.

PPM Language

Without a common language that can be used to communicate the PPM concepts, the principles will not be achieved. Some of these terms include:

Ownership: vision, message

Leverage: lever, constraint, critical chain, impact chain, pacing resource

Priorities: multitasking, single-tasking, sequence, focus, percent task impact

Status: remaining duration, done, buffer consumption

Planning: task, resource, duration, buffer size, project, program, portfolio

Uncertainty: project buffer, feeding buffer, focused duration, low-risk duration, commitment date, stretch goal, probability

Tools

This book covers a number of important tools, including:

- The PPM Pilot
- Single-project scheduling
- Buffer indicators
- Network building
- Measurements
- Resource management
- Multi-project scheduling
- Program management

Change Using the Cycle of Results™

The Cycle of Results is fundamental to the PPM change management approach. Applied in small and large ways across the implementation, it consists of the following basic pieces:

1. The central driver is the urgency to change; whether of an individual or a group.
2. We describe a vision to address that urgency, in order to set expectations.
3. We work with people to plan and create ownership, in order to develop commitment.
4. We implement the needed changes, in order to create value.
5. We measure results, in order to validate that the value was created.

6. We communicate, reevaluate, and reinforce the results achieved, in order to manage expectations and the implementation plan going forward.

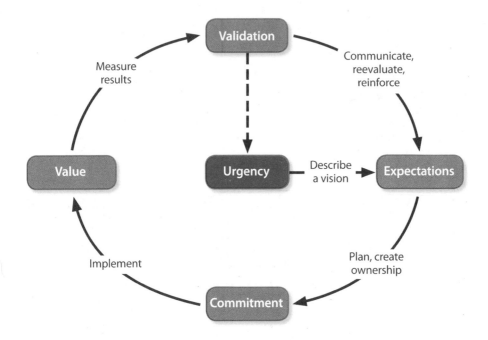

Behaviors

Various changes to work behaviors are discussed throughout the text. They fall into categories, notably:

- Project updating
- Relay race
- Communication
- Work rules
- Methodology transfer

APPENDIX B:
OLD GAME/NEW GAME

Introduction

Proponents of critical chain scheduling claim the power to revolutionize project management. They claim phenomenal results across many industries; some say it is the most significant new idea in project management in the last forty years.[1] And yet, in the "body of knowledge" documents of international professional organizations, project scheduling is acknowledged to be only a small piece of what project management is about. Just as a revolution in a small country may not even make the newspapers in a larger country, critical chain scheduling may seem insignificant next to the range of problems faced by management. In other words, what's the big deal?

To answer this question, it's first important to acknowledge that in the project world there is frequently a gap between two different realities: the reality of senior leaders who determine project requirements such as needed project completion dates, and the reality of the project team, those who need to supervise and conduct the project work. Typically the project manager and team members are stuck trying to resolve an impossible conflict—the "reality gap" between what is possible and what is required.

There are two ways to resolve this reality gap; we call them the "Old Game" and the "New Game." I'll start by discussing the Old Game, which is how the project scheduling game is played in most large organizations today. This game results directly in a lack of credible project planning, which in turn leads to miscommunication and poor decision-making. Middle managers are left in a "zone of reconciliation," having somehow to reconcile dreams and reality through heroic efforts and creative storytelling.

In the New Game, credible critical chain schedules are fundamental to good communication and are therefore a key to playing well. However, the New Game can't be played merely through scheduling; it requires process, discipline, and cooperation. When played properly, it results in a "zone of facilitation" across the entire organization, in which stakeholders at all levels and functions work together to achieve excellent project results.[2]

The Old Game

The standard process I've seen for creating and using schedules (a.k.a. "The Old Game") typically starts with requirements and dates. This information comes from senior leadership and/or marketing, based on business requirements. In environments where schedules are created, the project manager then works with individuals to create a schedule that meets the requirements and the date. If there is an apparent conflict, the project manager prepares a position and negotiates with senior leadership to get something he or she thinks the team needs.[3] This will usually be to relieve one or more of the big three constraints: resources, time, and scope. This flow is shown in figure B.1.

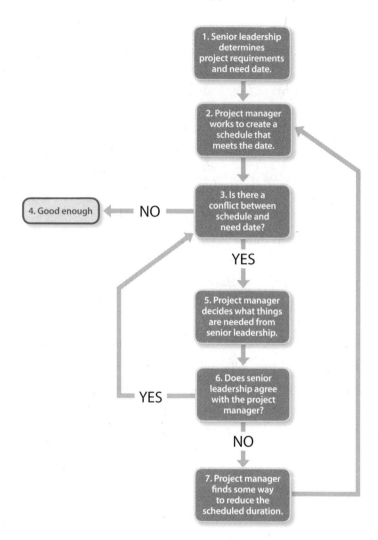

Figure B.1. "Old Game" playing board

Rules of the Old Game

Organizations play the Old Game by putting new projects on box 1 and moving them to box 4 as quickly and painlessly as possible.

The fundamental rule for everyone is individual survival, but there are other rules that vary from company to company. For example:

- If the requirements in box 1 are not impossible, management is being too easy.
- In performing box 2, the project manager should avoid clarification of requirements. If you don't want to know the answer, don't ask the question.
- The meaning of box 3, "Is there a conflict between schedule and need date?" depends on what "is" is.
- In box 5, ask for as much as you can, because you will get less than you ask for.
- Schedule credibility is irrelevant. The project manager should find the easiest possible way through box 7.

When playing the Old Game, it's common to put as many projects in play as possible. Often those projects assume availability of the same resources at the same time. There may be many projects that management doesn't even know about. As a result, most organizations seem to have far more projects in process than they can effectively work.

Note that boxes 1 and 6 are key control points for senior leadership. These are the points where leaders attempt to hold the line on resource use and project outcome. Managers, when presented with an alternative to the Old Game, often want to know, "If I'm sure the schedule is possible, how can I be sure people have an incentive to work as hard as they can?"[4]

Winning and Losing

People can grow to be very skilled at the Old Game. They achieve organizational stature from their ability to win. Senior leaders can win by pushing people to do more and more with less and less.

Project managers can win by keeping something in reserve, always having tricks up their sleeves; or by moving on before the major problems surface.

Unfortunately, the three major project constraints are really four: time, cost, scope, and credibility. If the apparent conflicts between the team's perception and the business needs can't be adequately resolved, the project manager is put in a position where "unwarranted optimism" is the only answer. In some organizations this is the first order of business: the schedule will meet the mandated dates, whether or not the project team believes that makes any sense. This process produces a schedule that is missing several key components, such as:

- Credibility: People experience tremendous pressure to sacrifice honesty for expedience. As a result, few if any believe what the schedule is telling them.
- Communication: Without a solid, credible foundation for communicating project status and needs, no one has reasonable data with which to make decisions. Decisions must therefore be made based on intuition and hope.
- Trust: The Old Game tends to create an adversarial relationship between senior leadership and the project personnel. Senior leadership wants an earlier date and tends not to believe the project team's claims. The project team comes to believe that senior leadership isn't listening.
- Ownership: With lack of trust comes lack of ownership. The different players no longer feel that it is their responsibility to create success. The project manager tends to focus on arguments rather than results. The project team as a whole looks for excuses. Senior leadership becomes frustrated and less and less willing to help.

Over the long term, this lack of trust and ownership means that often project managers and team members are not contributing as effectively as they could. It also means that senior leadership is not supporting their efforts well. Often the project team's only viable decision is to work harder, while never finding the time to work smarter. The Old Game results in frustration, mistrust, and poor decisions. People struggle against one another rather than against the real problems. In the end, project performance suffers and everyone loses.

It's no wonder that predictability and visibility are so important to senior management. In our experience, most executives will put project predictability before speed on their organizational wish lists. This is a symptom of their lack of confidence and control. And yet the game that they and their people play virtually forces project communication that lacks visibility and predictive value.

The New Game

The "New Game" is played on the board shown in figure B.2. First we describe the game board, then the new rules.

1. Senior leadership determines project requirements and business needs

"Project requirements" describe what the project needs to accomplish (what is "done"). "Business needs" include a description of why the requirements must be accomplished (what is the value to the company), when the project must be finished (the business need date), and the importance of the need date. This information should be well understood by the project team and written into a project charter that is approved by senior leadership; otherwise project teams may work hard to meet requirements that are not

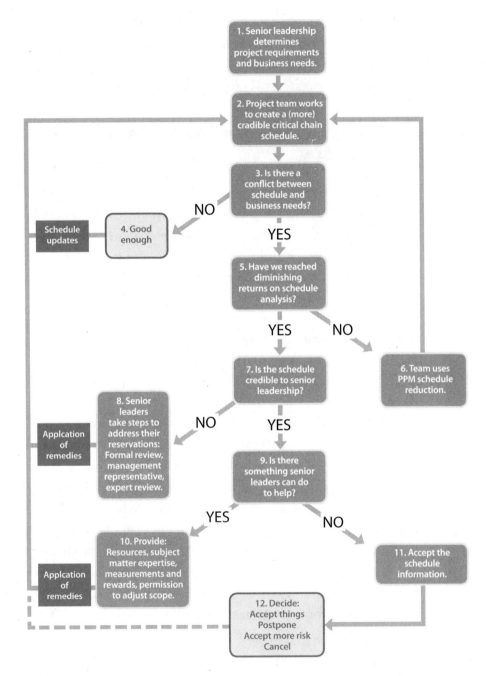

Figure B.2. "New Game" playing board

significant and ignore requirements that are crucial. "Business needs" may include budgetary considerations. Depending on the organization's gating processes, there may also be a feasibility phase during which a rough initial project schedule is created.

2. Project team works to create a (more) credible critical chain schedule

The project team must work together cross-functionally to create a unified picture of how the project charter will be carried out. The key is to have a credible departure point for analysis and decision-making. The initial schedule may or may not meet the date dictated by business need. Credibility can be defined as playing by the New Game rules, including:

- The project team is trying to present an honest picture.
- Risks are taken into account.
- Business objectives are taken into account.

Critical chain scheduling is the simplest, most reliable method I know of for creating credible schedules, both for single and multiple projects. Taking into account resource contention is an important part of the critical chain approach and certainly promotes realism. But the critical chain approach to protecting the schedule is essential to credibility. The traditional safety time put into task duration estimates to protect the completion of individual tasks is often "incredible," kind of like mandatory salary increases in contracts. Taking it out is unacceptable to workers, leaving it in doesn't work for management. With the critical chain "buffer" concept, the safety time is taken out of the individual tasks and put back into the project plan in strategic locations as "buffers." By managing this safety explicitly in buffers we still have protection, but it belongs to everyone. Everyone can see it and evaluate its use.

We can track overall project progress much more effectively through consumption of buffers, and *everyone believes the results*. We have stable project schedules and predictable project outcomes. You could say that buffers move the focus of credibility from individual tasks ("I really need to get this task done on time") to the project ("we really need to get this project done on time"). Some tasks will be early and some late, and this is expected; the project itself is very likely to be completed by the commitment date. Therefore the project schedule is truly credible.

As the New Game is played with more and more projects, it also becomes more and more important to understand inter-project relationships. Therefore credibility may also require taking into account the impact of multiple projects on shared resources, shared integration points, and relative project priorities.

3. Is there a conflict between schedule and business needs?

The team must analyze whether the schedule is in conflict with the business needs. As part of the analysis they need to resolve any lack of clarity with those needs. This question may require a review by senior leadership, especially if the schedule is ready for acceptance (i.e. there's no conflict).

4. Good Enough

Declaring "good enough" is always "for now." Initially, the project team should brief senior leadership so that leaders understand and approve the decision to move ahead with the schedule. The line from box 4 back to box 2 indicates that the schedule will always be under examination for improvements or needed changes. The "Schedule updates" note on the arrow out of box 4 implies that the schedule must stay credible; that is, it must be kept up-to-date.

5. Have we reached diminishing returns on schedule analysis?

Project teams sometimes have a tendency to spin their wheels, unable to resolve the conflict between business needs and their perception of reality. There are many ways to help teams challenge their assumptions, such as:

- Ask, "If you could do whatever you wanted, with no resource or policy restrictions, what would you do differently?" This may result in the need for help from senior leadership, meaning you must first pass through boxes 7 to 10.
- Check the practices of other companies or groups inside the company.
- Provide an outside expert to review assumptions.

6. Team uses critical chain tools to reduce the schedule duration.

A focused analysis approach using critical chain software allows easy identification of those tasks, links, and resources that are causing the project schedule to be as long as it is. Team members challenge one another's assumptions to reduce project schedules. During this process it is important to have a cross-functional team that is familiar with both the critical chain concepts and the project itself.

As usual, credibility must be maintained throughout.

7. Is the schedule credible to senior leadership?

Assuming the team has been careful to maintain a credible schedule, and the schedule doesn't yet meet business needs, we must be sure that senior leadership buys into the current picture. That doesn't mean it's the final schedule and it doesn't mean they acknowledge that it is telling any final truth. It does mean the assumptions behind the schedule are understood well enough that senior leadership believes that—barring significant further interventions or understanding—the schedule is realistic. It means that senior people are willing to work with the project team in a non-adversarial way, with the schedule as a point of departure.

8. Senior leaders takes steps to address their reservations

If senior leaders don't believe the project team, whose problem is it? The common answer, the Old Game answer, is "the other guy's." That effectively blocks further communication because *the project team is already stuck*. Realistically, they are likely to teleport over to box 7 of the Old Game. They need help, not more pressure.

There are a number of steps senior leadership can take to put their concerns to rest, such as:

- Hold a formal schedule review to discuss schedule assumptions.
- Put a trusted management or customer representative on the project team.
- Have an outside expert evaluate the current project plan and make suggestions.

9. Is there something Senior Leadership can do to help?

Think of things that senior leadership might be able to do or supply that will help complete a project sooner. Many possibilities should be considered, for example:

- More or better resources.
- Bringing in outside subject matter experts.

- Changes to measurements and rewards (e.g. team incentives, spot bonuses, overtime pay).
- Granting permission to adjust scope.
- Help in finding better ways to allow people to be more fully engaged in their work (e.g. quiet places to work).
- Making sure the project will have sufficiently high priority.
- Expedited review and action on buffer recovery plans.

Some of these ideas, such as measurements and better work engagement, might profitably become a more global part of the workplace.

10. Senior leadership provides help

It's one thing to commit resources or other help when the project is being scheduled; it can be quite another to provide that help when the time comes. If the help is not provided, the assumptions behind the schedule are invalidated and the team's commitment (the schedule) becomes unfeasible. This is true of behavior changes as well as resources. For example, suppose team members are encouraged to stick to their priorities and say "no" to lower-priority work. If senior leaders criticize them for that, the desired behavior change (staying on-task) is undermined. Any scheduling assumptions dependent on that behavior, such as "no multitasking," may become invalid.

11. Accept the schedule information

There comes a point where further discussion appears fruitless. Everyone concerned must accept that the schedule is as good as it's going to get, at least for now. Senior leadership must make a decision. Sometimes this isn't easy, but "no decision" is often a bad decision.

12. Make a decision about the project

Senior leadership, with support from the project team and information from the schedule, must choose from among several possible alternatives, for example:

- Accept the timing: allow the project commitment date to be later than the declared business need. Even here, all is not lost; the team may continue to find ways to improve the situation.
- Postpone: put the project on hold while working on better opportunities and/or looking for partners, technology improvements, etc.
- Accept more risk: In a critical chain world, it is possible to operate with less protection time. That is typically done by sliding the project buffer to the left, so that it begins partially consumed. This must be done infrequently and managed carefully. Otherwise, in addition to greater risk that the project will be late, there is a huge risk that project teams will begin to regard critical chain scheduling as just another management attempt to squeeze them. That, in turn, will cause people to revert to the Old Game.
- Outsource significant parts of the project: this is obviously only effective if the outsourcing partner can actually help speed up the project.
- Re-scope the project.
- Cancel the project.

Rules of the New Game

The object of the New Game is to get bottom-line results for the organization while maintaining credibility, communication, trust, and ownership. We may get to box 4 or box 12, but even with a "good enough" schedule the journey is far from over.

The New Game has several rules:

1. *Insist upon honesty*; that is the only basis for long-term trust. All players should give realistic need dates, requirements, task times, and so on.
2. *Need can't win over reality.* Denial takes you back to the Old Game. Senior leadership may not say, "This schedule is unacceptable" without being willing to consider alternatives. Project managers and team members should be rewarded, not punished, for reporting what they believe to be the truth.
3. *Account for risks.* No significant increase of risk (or decrease of buffer) is allowed to meet dates without being explicit about the magnitude of the risk, mitigation plans, and contingency plans.
4. All players should be asking, "*How can I help?*" Everyone should be focused on helping achieve the business results.
5. *Focus on real business objectives.* Don't add task due dates to put more pressure on people; don't build grudges or ill will.
6. *Use the process* on the game board. For example, doing anything without clarifying the needs of the business (box 1) is a mistake. How can the team make effective tradeoffs without a good understanding of the business needs? Jumping to senior leadership help (boxes 9-10) before establishing credibility (boxes 7-8) is a mistake. Leadership should never invest in a project when they don't believe the data justify the investment.
7. *Hold people accountable* for following the rules.

"But wait," you may be asking. "If this revolutionary critical chain approach produces shorter schedules, why do we even need boxes 7 to 12? In fact, why do we need to play the New Game at all?"

Applied properly, the critical chain approach produces shorter *credible* schedules. Projects are completed much more quickly *relative to what would have happened otherwise*. The schedules may or may not be shorter relative to the dates and schedules that arise from the Old Game. If you apply critical chain scheduling and a schedule is perceived as too long, you must proceed to box 7. Otherwise you will be back to the Old Game.

B.5 Winning With the New Game

The New Game is not about heroism and individual valor; it is about people working together to achieve great results. Even "ordinary" project managers can play the New Game with extraordinary success. Winning must be expressed in terms of stakeholders achieving what they need. By winning with the New Game, the organization builds a culture that values things important to its long-term success, such as:

- Credibility: Not only is the project schedule credible, but the team is more credible to itself and to senior leadership.
- Communication: The schedule gives a basis for all project stakeholders to communicate effectively about the project and its requirements.
- Trust: Through good communication, senior leadership and team members build trust and overcome years of poor communication and dysfunctional coping mechanisms.
- Ownership: When all the key players have a say in what the project is and how it shall be executed, and when they trust that the commitments are possible, they develop phenomenal ownership and team spirit.

One functional manager, after trying the New Game, said, "For the first time, I really believe what the schedule is telling me. This is the first time that I've ever felt like we really have a chance to make it." A senior leader who learned to play the New Game well said, "I can talk to teams using ProChain, ask questions and get real answers. When there is a delay, they know what is causing it. The conversations don't break down to guessing and defensiveness the way they used to." These are typical comments, but they are not a result of scheduling alone. They are a result of effectively integrating scheduling into the organization's business processes—the New Game.

B.6 Conclusions

The Old Game comes about through both the lack of credible schedules and the lack of good processes for using them to analyze and communicate effectively. All the standard complaints about

TABLE 6	Comparison of old and new games	
CHARACTERISTIC	**OLD GAME**	**NEW GAME**
Value from schedules	Minimal	Predictability, visibility
Schedule credibility	Low; planning is often abandoned as a waste of time	High; credibility is a requirement of the New Game
Communication	Poor, due to dependence on intuition and poor data	Honest, based on a shared perception of reality
Trust	Low	High
Ownership	Low	High
Triple constraint (time, resources, scope)	Often violated	Seldom violated
Reality gap	Significant	Closed

project results—late, over budget, under scope, mistrust, burned out people, and on and on—are also standard outcomes of the Old Game.

The New Game bridges the reality gap between business desires and project reality. It produces results vastly superior to those of the Old Game, as shown in table 6.

The results of ProChain Project Management approach plus the New Game have the power to revolutionize project management in any project organization.

GLOSSARY

Buffer: Time strategically put into the schedule to protect against unanticipated delays, and to allow for early starts. Buffers are not slack; they are essential parts of the schedule. There are two main types of buffer: Project Buffers, which protect project commitment date(s); and Feeding Buffers, which protect projects' critical chains.

Buffer management: The PPM process by which project status can be monitored, assessed, and communicated. It includes project execution and control mechanisms. Buffer management provides the means to give relative priorities to tasks, based on their impact on projects' completions. The relative task priorities can be reflected by the Percent Task Impact parameter. Buffer management can also be used to look ahead and predict the effects of schedule disruptions on the projects as a whole in order to evaluate potential problems and to respond more quickly and effectively.

Business need date: The date the business needs for a particular project to be completed. It is typically determined by management.

Check tasks: The tasks that currently cause a buffer to be used up; they are therefore the tasks that need to be checked to explain buffer consumption.

Checklist survey: A ProChain tool that helps to monitor various processes used during project scheduling and execution.

Critical chain: The set of tasks that determines overall project duration(s). Usually it requires taking resource capacity into account. It is typically regarded as the major constraint for a project.

Duck farming: A management technique that involves force-feeding people with unrealistic expectations, in the hope that they will thereby be more productive.

Enterprise project management (EPM): A system designed to manage projects and resources across an organization. It may include Project Portfolio Management (another PPM) and various aspects of Product Lifecycle Management (PLM).

Enterprise resource planning (ERP): An enterprise-wide system typically intended to integrate an organization's data systems. This integration may include many component systems, such as customer management, finance, manufacturing, and human resources.

Focused duration: An "average" task duration that assumes no multitasking.

Gating task: A task that has not yet been started and that has no predecessors; it "gates" the flow of work into the organization.

Impact chain: The most limiting chain of tasks feeding a given task or buffer, considering both resource and task dependencies. For a task, the impact chain shows which predecessors prevent the task from moving earlier; for a buffer, it shows which tasks are causing the current level of consumption. When you have multiple projects linked together, the impact chain may span multiple projects.

Individual contributor (IC): An individual who is responsible for hands-on project work.

Low-risk (high-confidence) duration: A task has a high probability (typically 90 to 95 percent) of being completed within its "low-risk" duration. This value is used by ProChain software to help set buffer sizes.

Milestone: A specific event or achievement in a project. For scheduling purposes, milestones are usually associated with dates.

Moving finish line: This syndrome involves frequently moving the commitment date for a project, in order to accommodate changes to the project's status. Occasionally it is legitimate to change the finish line, but often this approach is used to artificially improve on-time performance.

Multitasking: A practice of interrupting work on one task in order to work on another task. It results from giving people more than one task to do at the same time, without them following clear and consistent priorities among those tasks. Among many drawbacks, it usually results in people taking much longer than necessary to complete every task, which means long project durations.

Multitasking maelstrom: The chaotic environment that results from rampant multitasking.

Network: A plan that combines resource information (such as people, functions, and calendars) and task information (such as durations, resources, and linkages between tasks) in a way that shows how we plan to fulfill the project objectives.

Network build team (NBT): A team of individuals that participates in the creation and maintenance of a PPM schedule for a given project, and helps align the project team and management with that schedule. It usually consists of the project manager(s) as well as key resource managers and individual contributors.

Percent task impact (PTI): This value is calculated by ProChain software to show a task's influence on a corresponding project buffer. The value's intended use is to help resources and resource managers prioritize tasks. A number equal to the project buffer's current consumption indicates that the task is on the project buffer's impact chain. A higher number typically indicates that the task should be given higher priority.

PPM pilot: A trial of a particular tool or methodology. A PPM pilot is a trial of PPM, both to show the level of improvement that is possible and to learn about the organization. It usually consists of one or more project launches.

PPM rollout: The process of rolling out the PPM methodology to an entire organization.

ProChain Enterprise (PCE): ProChain Enterprise is a web-based project and portfolio reporting and tracking tool that interfaces with ProChain Project Scheduling and ProChain Pipeline to improve dramatically project management capabilities across multi-level and geographically dispersed organizations.

ProChain Expert Certification: A rigorous process used by ProChain to certify individuals as fully qualified to use, teach, and mentor the different elements of PPM.

ProChain Pipeline (PCP): ProChain Pipeline software enables a user to effectively analyze and appropriately pace projects for an organization based on its critical chain schedules. ProChain Pipeline contains tools and reports that aid a master scheduler in the management of multiple projects. It is designed to facilitate the collection and dissemination of information important to senior managers, resource managers, and project managers. ProChain Pipeline software facilitates the institutionalization of PPM across an organization.

ProChain Project Management (PPM): A project management methodology developed by ProChain Solutions, Inc. to convert the theoretical concepts like critical chain into a practical set of tools, processes, policies, and procedures for managing projects.

ProChain Project Scheduling (PPS): This software enables a user to effectively schedule and apply buffer management to individual projects on the desktop using the PPM methodology.

Program: Traditionally, a program is a group of projects interrelated in a way that achieves one or more large-scale organizational objectives. In other words, a program is a very complex project.

Project charter: This document describes various aspects of a project. The document may include project objectives, key personnel, requirements, and so on. It may be used to give a project manager authority to use organizational resources. In PPM, it is also used as a common starting point for project scheduling.

Project launch: A soup-to-nuts PPM scheduling exercise with a single project team, from interviews and training to schedule creation to buffer updating.

Project Management Office (PMO): Also known as a Program Management Office. This is an organization responsible for project management excellence. In a PPM implementation, active certified experts and certification candidates are often part of a PMO.

Projected times: Task start and finish times calculated by ProChain software, representing the times that the task is projected to start and finish if all goes well. Tasks with no predecessors that have not been started are assumed to start no earlier than their scheduled or "gating" times; tasks with predecessors are assumed to start as early as possible, taking into account resource contention.

Schedule: We try to distinguish between a plan, which could encompass many aspects of project management (including the Project Charter), and the schedule, which is a model of the project work that produces dates (in particular, for PPM, commitment dates).

Schedule Chicken: A game whose object is not to be the first to admit you're going to miss a due date. The first to admit to a delay gets the blame; the others, by having more time in which to complete their work, get the benefit of the delay.

Single-tasking: The opposite of multitasking; namely the practice of focusing on one task at a time—until that task is complete—before moving on to the next task.

Steering Team: A group of executives responsible and ultimately accountable for making sure the PPM implementation stays on track. They are responsible for approving and nurturing the vision for the implementation.

Task Engagement: The opposite of multitasking, an alignment of focus and attention on individual tasks. Task engagement is achieved when people concentrate, focus, and/or are absorbed by the task. Common synonyms for task engagement are concentration, flow, "in the zone," and attentiveness. Significant productivity, task quality, and quality of work life improvements can be achieved when people start to practice task engagement.

Task manager: The person responsible to the Project Manager for ensuring that a task or group of tasks will be delivered as required.

Touch time: The amount of time spent in actual hands-on work for a task. Ideally, focused durations should consist entirely of estimated touch time.

Vision: Every PPM implementation needs a shared vision to create alignment around where it is going and why. The vision provides a consistent way to talk about what people are trying to achieve and it sets a clear direction for the organization.

Zone of Reconciliation: The zone in the organizational pyramid responsible for reconciling the expectations of leadership with the on-the-ground realities of the individual contributors and project work.

NOTES

Preface

1. Robert C. Newbold, *Project Management in the Fast Lane* (Boca Raton: St. Lucie Press, 1998).

Introduction

1. Brian Tippett, "Critical Chain Implementation" (ProChain Conference, 2004).
2. Douglas R. Brandt, "A New Vision for Project Management," *Cutter IT Journal*, March 2003, 19–23.
3. Doug Foster, "CCPM in Large Program Environments" (ProChain Conference, 2006).
4. Rich Gargas, "Rx for Implementation Success: Rolling Out Critical Chain Project Management in a Large IT Organization" (ProChain Conference, 2007).
5. Jason Bork, "Execute Better Than Our Competitors" (ProChain Conference, 2008).
6. Sometimes cited as just time, cost, and quality. PRINCE2 talks about time, cost, scope, quality, risk, and benefit. See *Managing Successful Projects with PRINCE2 3rd edition,* (London: Office of Government Commerce, 2002), 223–224.

7. ". . . when leaders become confused and allow the deployment of the means for improvement to become the strategic objective of improvement, then the effort is more likely to fail than to succeed." Raymond C. Floyd, *A Culture of Rapid Improvement: Creating and Sustaining an Engaged Workforce* (Boca Raton: CRC Press, 2008), 28. This is an important book by someone who has successfully practiced culture change from within large organizations.

Chapter 1

1. Tom DeMarco, *Slack*, (New York: Broadway Books, 2001), 81.
2. The ProChain software, along with the principles on which it is based, has been adopted by thousands of companies across seven continents to manage projects in many fields, including high-tech, drug development, construction, and defense.
3. You can look, for example, at http://www.innovation.org/index. cfm/InsideDrugDiscovery (accessed January 30, 2008) for descriptions of the development process. It's generally estimated that a single approved new drug requires researching 5,000 to 10,000 compounds. If a funnel representing the winnowing process for a single new drug were a foot wide at the bottom, it would be over a mile wide at the top.
4. For one overview of the state of the pharmaceutical industry, see Barbara Martinez and Jacob Goldstein, "Big Pharma Faces Grim Prognosis," *The Wall Street Journal*, December 6, 2007, http://online.wsj.com/public/article_print/SB119689933952615133.html (accessed January 17, 2008).
5. The risks of drug development can especially be seen in the biotechnology area, where public companies showed an aggregate loss of more than 7 percent in 2006, up from about 6 percent in 2005. See *Beyond Borders: Global Biotechnology Report 2007* (EYGM Limited, 2007), p.7.

Chapter 2

1. This book does not provide a guide to writing vision statements. Kotter is one good source of advice, for example: John P. Kotter, *Leading Change* (Boston, MA: Harvard Business School Press, 1996) or John P. Kotter and Dan S. Cohen, *The Heart of Change* (Boston, MA: Harvard Business School Press, 2002).
2. See *A Guide to the Project Management Body of Knowledge*, Third Edition (Newtown Square, PA: Project Management Institute, 2004). You can obtain various body-of-knowledge documents from the Association for Project Management at www.apm.org.uk, the Project Management Institute at www.pmi.org, and the International Project Management Association at www.ipma.ch.

Chapter 3

1. The term "Pareto Principle," named after the Italian economist Vilfredo Pareto, is attributed to Dr. Joseph Juran.
2. See Newbold, *Project Management in the Fast Lane*, 139–141.
3. That "certain point" is discussed in Frederick P. Brooks Jr., *The Mythical Man-Month: Essays on Software Engineering Anniversary Edition* (Reading, MA: Addison-Wesley Publishing Company, 1995). It is common to assume that more people equals more speed, while often the opposite is true.
4. This concept is fundamental to the Theory of Constraints (TOC), of which critical chain scheduling is one piece. There are numerous introductory TOC books on the market, but you can't do better than to start with Eliyahu M. Goldratt and Jeff Cox, *The Goal, 3rd edition* (North River Press: Croton-on-Hudson, 2004).
5. For an interesting but somewhat dated survey of TOC literature and results, see Victoria J. Mabin and Steven J. Balderstone, *The*

World of the Theory of Constraints: A Review of the International Literature (Boca Raton: St. Lucie Press, 1999).

6. Note that the investor pressure would create urgency to change. The need for urgency as a driver of change is discussed in Chapter 15.

Chapter 4

1. You can decide whether this requirement is due to union rules or management requirements.
2. Peter Drucker's 1966 classic *The Effective Executive* has a great discussion of priorities and focused time. Peter F. Drucker, *The Effective Executive* (New York: HarperCollins, 1966), see especially Chapter 2.
3. Mihaly Csikszentmihalyi, *Flow: The Psychology of Optimal Experience* (New York: HarperCollins, 1990).
4. If you carry out the calculations, you'll find that the thirteenth project will take over four more years to complete. Of course, the project could complete in two months, if you ignored all the other projects. Now suppose you kept all the projects active and just changed the rules. What would happen if you stopped the multitasking and focused on each project, in sequence, until it was done? Project thirteen would then finish in only fourteen more months—three and a half times as quickly.
5. See for example Jonathan Spira, "The High Cost of Interruptions," http://www.kmworld.com/Articles/ReadArticle.aspx?Article ID=14543 (accessed October 14, 2007).
6. "The brain cannot multitask." John Medina, *Brain Rules* (Seattle: Pear Press, 2008), 84.

Chapter 5

1. This is translated and quoted by Andrew E. Kramer, "Yes, a Lot of People Died, But . . .," *New York Times,* August 12, 2007. Also available online at http://www.nytimes.com/2007/08/12/weekinreview/12kramer.html.
2. Duck Farming is closely related to "Theory X," as described in Douglas McGregor's 1960 classic *The Human Side of Enterprise.* Theory X says that the average worker inherently dislikes work, and that therefore fear and force are essential to good management. Douglas McGregor, *The Human Side of Enterprise Annotated Edition* (New York: McGraw Hill, 2006). Duck Farming remains popular even in organizations that claim to reject Theory X.
3. For an extensive discussion of what I call "Duck Farming," see DeMarco, *Slack,* Chapters 7 and 8.

Chapter 6

1. Referring to a survey of high-performing "Alpha" project managers: "Alphas allocated just over twice as much time toward project planning as their counterparts." Andy Crowe, *Alpha Project Managers: What the Top 2 Percent Know That Everyone Else Does Not,* Velociteach Press, October 2006, 107. A survey of 100 project managers cited by PMI indicates that the top two project success factors are "PM planning and procedures" and "communications." See Alistair Taylor and CIO Canada, "Increasing IT Project Success for Project Managers and their Clients," http://www.pmi.org/PDF/pp_taylor.pdf (accessed September 9, 2007). And so on.
2. Stephen R. Covey, *The Seven Habits of Highly Effective People* (New York: Simon & Schuster, 1989), 151.

3. Barry W. Boehm and Philip N. Papaccio, "Understanding and Controlling Software Costs," IEEE Transactions on Software Engineering 14, no. 10 (October 1988), 1466.
4. See Newbold, *Project Management in the Fast Lane*, 102.

Chapter 7

1. DeMarco and Lister list ten, each of which can affect time or cost, including Requirements, Changing Environment, Resources, Politics, and Innovation. Tom DeMarco and Timothy Lister, *Waltzing with Bears* (New York: Dorset House Publishing, 2003), 24.
2. See Chapter 10 for the answer.
3. The term "deadline" comes from prisons in the American Civil War, where stepping past the deadline literally meant death. It seems likely that sensible people left a little extra space between themselves and the line.

Chapter 8

1. "It is important that wine tasters develop an extensive odor vocabulary to accurately express their perceptions [. . .]. In contrast, the terms most consumers use to describe a wine express more their emotional response to the wine than its sensory attributes." Ronald S. Jackson, *Wine Tasting: A Professional Handbook* (San Diego: Elsevier Academic Press, 2002), 57. For an interesting article from the New Yorker magazine on the relationships between language and culture in the Parahã tribe of Brazil, in particular discussing tribal memory and ability to accept new ideas, see http://www.newyorker.com/reporting/2007/04/16/070416fa_fact_colapinto (accessed November 21, 2007).

2. David Hanna likes to quote Arthur W. Jones, "All organizations are perfectly designed to get the results they get." See for example David P. Hanna, *Leadership for the Ages* (Provo, UT: Executive Excellence Publishing, 2001), 163.

Chapter 9

1. There are a few "standard" references, in particular: Eliyahu M. Goldratt, *Critical Chain* (Great Barrington, MA: North River Press, 1997); Newbold, *Project Management in the Fast Lane*; and Lawrence P. Leach, *Critical Chain Project Management, Second Edition* (Norwood, MA: Artech House Publishers, 2004).
2. The ProChain software does allow for different definitions of the critical chain, in order to deal with certain exceptional circumstances.
3. Other types of buffers mentioned in various places; resource buffers, pacing resource or "drum resource" buffers, and "capacity buffers" are a few. We do not find these concepts to be nearly as useful as the basic project and feeding buffers, and therefore only teach them in specific circumstances. You can find out more by consulting Newbold, *Project Management in the Fast Lane*, or Leach, *Critical Chain Project Management, Second Edition*.
4. Tom DeMarco suggests that a project needs to have both goals and estimates, and that they should be different. See Tom DeMarco, *The Deadline* (New York: Dorset House Publishing, 1997), 302.
5. Some blue-sky R&D projects have huge amounts of uncertainty. David Anderson gives some guidelines for buffer sizing with software projects; see David J. Anderson, *Agile Management for Software Engineering: Applying the Theory of Constraints for Business Results* (Upper Saddle River, NJ: Prentice Hall, 2004), chap. 4. DeMarco and Lister speak of a "window of uncertainty," and suggest that, "For the software industry as a whole, window size is in the range of 150 to 200 percent of N," where N is the

time from project start to earliest possible delivery. DeMarco and Lister, *Waltzing with Bears*, 59.

6. Clay Geran, "The Abbott Diagnostics Division Project Management Office Keys to Sustained Success" (ProChain Conference, 2006).

7. The formula would be (low risk – focused) × buffer percentage.

8. Newbold, *Project Management in the Fast Lane*, 94–95.

9. For those familiar with these approaches, note that a basic assumption for using the Central Limit Theorem—independence of the tasks—is clearly violated in a project plan. The tasks are very much interdependent, through shared objectives and resources.

10. Answer: $(0.5)^{10}$, which is just under 0.1 percent.

Chapter 10

1. See, for example, Lawrence P. Leach, *Lean Project Management: Eight Principles for Success* (amazon.com: BookSurge Publishing, 2006), 203.

2. Stuff happens. Also see the Beer Game, described in Peter M. Senghe, *The Fifth Discipline* (New York: Doubleday/Currency, 1990), chap. 3. Deming discusses the dangers of overadjustment using his funnel experiment, see for example W. Edwards Deming, *Out of the Crisis* (Cambridge, MA: MIT CAES, 1986), 327 and following.

Chapter 11

1. We've seen individual critical chain plans that have 10,000 tasks. Such plans tend to be very painful to use for analysis; it's hard to get the big picture. They can also take a great deal of time to maintain. If significant detail is truly needed, I recommend using the program management approach described in Chapter 13 to break your project plan into manageable pieces.

2. Julie Cameron and Allen Warren, "Calculating the ROI for Project Cancellations" (ProChain Conference, 2004).

3. See, for example, *A Guide to the Project Management Body of Knowledge* or *Project Delivery: A System and Process for Benchmark Performance* (Denver, CO: CH2M Hill, 2000), 73.

4. This example comes from Stephen Carl Cook, "Applying *Critical Chain* to Improving the Management of Uncertainty in Projects," a paper in partial fulfillment of the requirements for an MBA and MS in EE at the Massachusetts Institute of Technology, 1998.

5. See *A Guide to the Project Management Body of Knowledge*, 144; or many other references.

6. Habit 2 in Covey, *The Seven Habits of Highly Effective People*, 151.

7. See, for example, Goldratt, *Critical Chain*, 66.

8. Once again, credibility and transparency are key. While a detailed discussion of network modeling is beyond the scope of this book, a couple of examples might help illustrate some pitfalls:

- Date constraints such as "must finish on" are often popular, but should be used with caution so that you don't create artificial and hard-to-understand restrictions in your network.
- Different types of task relationships, such as start-to-start, finish-to-finish, lag times, or lead times, can be very useful. They can also significantly decrease the clarity of a project network. If such links are substitutes for un-modeled tasks, you should make sure that the durations of lags or leads are appropriately modeled as focused time.

Chapter 12

1. Crowe notes the importance of making people aware of the value of project management in Crowe, *Alpha Project Managers: What the Top 2 Percent Know That Everyone Else Does Not*, 182.

2. Time saved for the projects can be compared with the time costs of the PPM process. While the comparative value of the implementation is usually a no-brainer, if you don't collect the data, people will sometimes remember the time they spent and forget about the benefits that resulted.

3. Brian Hobbs and Monique Aubry, "Identifying the Structure that Underlies the Extreme Variability Found Among PMOs" (Newtown Square, PA: Project Management Institute Research Conference 2006), 13.

4. In general: "EVM [Earned Value Management] should not be used as the basis of a reward scheme." Ray W. Stratton, *The Earned Value Management Maturity Model®* (Vienna, VA: Management Concepts, 2006), 61.

5. See, for example, Michael L. George, *Lean Six Sigma for Service* (New York: McGraw Hill, 2003), 281–289.

Chapter 13

1. I've already mentioned Tom DeMarco's *Slack*; see also Tom DeMarco and Timothy Lister, *Peopleware: Productive Projects and Teams, Second Edition* (New York: Dorset House Publishing Co., 1999), 67.

2. See Leach, *Critical Chain Project Management, Second Edition*, 141. Earned value data can be used to monitor cost buffers.

3. An early quote: "Typically, the company has in process twice as much work as it can staff effectively. This means that half the work is sitting idle somewhere, and each project takes twice as long as it needs to." Preston G. Smith, "Saying 'No' to Customers," *Across the Board*, March 1994, 56–57.

4. See Preston G. Smith and Donald G. Reinertsen, *Developing Products in Half the Time* (New York: John Wiley and Sons, Inc., 1998), chap. 11, especially p. 207. The book treats several of

the concepts discussed in this book, including milestones and delaying project starts.

5. For more selection criteria, see Newbold, *Project Management in the Fast Lane*, 154–155.

6. This seems to be standard across many consultants and industries, based on interviews I have conducted. It also seems to contradict standard critical chain theory as explained by many.

7. The network building process described in Chapter 11, especially the discussion of preparatory work, contains several elements of schedule design. When scheduling a large program, schedule design and "planning for the plan" become even more important. Before you start building the schedules, you need to understand how the schedule pieces will fit together and how they will be used and updated. See also Murray B. Woolf, *Faster Construction Projects with CPM Scheduling* (New York: McGraw-Hill, 2007), chap. 12.

8. We have used some of these techniques effectively. We never recommend using them in large organizations with R&D or new product development projects, because buy-in will be a huge problem. There are two associated effects that we have observed from non-ProChain implementations. On the one hand, such techniques can result in a complete failure of the implementation to take hold. On the other hand, they can also result in quick benefits, which can tempt people to ignore longer-term culture change issues. Unaddressed cultural problems will make the positive results more and more difficult to sustain over time.

Chapter 14

1. See, for example, Hiroyuki Hirano (translated by Bruce Talbot), *5 Pillars of the Visual Workplace* (Portland, OR: Productivity Press, 1995). 5S refers to five principles whose words—in

Japanese—start with the "S" sound. They are sometimes
translated into English as Organization, Orderliness, Cleanliness,
Standardization, and Discipline.

2. Metcalfe's Law, which states that the value of a network is
proportional to the square of the number of users, also seems
relevant to languages and change efforts.

3. For an example, look at Senge, *The Fifth Discipline*, 145–146
or 345. Or you can just search for "resistance to change" on
amazon.com.

4. For a great discussion of strategies people use in selling to one
another, see Robert B. Cialdini, *Influence: The Psychology of
Persuasion* (New York: William Morrow and Company, Inc.,
1993).

5. It's amusing to speculate how our species would fare if we were
not skeptical about sales. How would you decide what to buy or
for whom to vote?

6. These two considerations that cause resistance correspond
closely to the discussion of motivation and ability in Kerry
Patterson, Joseph Grenny, David Maxfield, Ron McMillan,
and Al Switzler, *Influencer: The Power to Change Anything* (New
York: McGraw-Hill, 2007), 77–81.

7. B. H. Liddell Hart, *Strategy, Second Revised Edition* (London:
Frederick A. Praeger, Inc., 1954), 20.

Chapter 15

1. Jeanie Duck calls the phase after "Implementation" in a change
process "Determination" (subtitled "When the Monster Rules
the Hallways"). The idea is that you need great determination
to see change efforts through to the point where the needed
changes have become the standard way of doing things. See
Jeanie Daniel Duck, *The Change Monster* (New York: Three
Rivers Press, 2001), part 5.

2. Or: ". . . change is about selling, not telling." For an interesting discussion of change, see Alan Deutschman, *Change or Die* (New York: HarperCollins Publishers Inc., 2007). The quote is from page 57.

3. This is a very brief discussion of a very broad topic. Many of these ideas on urgency and value can be seen in Keith M. Eades, *The New Solution Selling* (New York: McGraw Hill, 2004).

4. Or "Perpetual optimism is a force multiplier." Colin Powell, *My American Journey* (New York: Random House, 1995), 613.

5. Marketing guru Geoffrey Moore refers to this as the "Bowling Alley," where pins start to knock one another over. See Geoffrey A. Moore, *Inside the Tornado* (New York: HarperCollins, 1995), chap. 3.

6. Eades in *The New Solution Selling* talks a great deal about pain rather than urgency, because pain tends to be more concrete, and most often the urgency to change is caused by some kind of pain. Note that all the listed examples refer to some kind of pain. Kotter refers instead to urgency; see Kotter, *Leading Change*, chap. 3.

Chapter 16

1. Some of Michael Gerber's books have good discussions of "process," especially the earlier ones; for example, Michael E. Gerber, *The E-Myth Revisited* (New York: Harper Collins, 1995). The Software Engineering Institute's integrated capability maturity model (CMMI, see http://www.sei.cmu.edu/cmmi/) is all about process, and the higher levels build in more and more ability to adapt processes to the changing needs of the business.

2. Those who don't want to repeat the past are condemned to remember it. Also those who do want to repeat the past.

3. The names of the company and VP have been changed.

4. The importance to learning of repetition spaced out over time is also known as the "spacing effect." This effect is well documented; see for example Medina, *Brain Rules*, 132–146 or http://www.wired.com/medtech/health/magazine/16-05/ff_wozniak (accessed 14 August 2008).

5. This relates directly to Kotter's concept of the "Guiding Coalition;" Kotter, *Leading Change*, chap. 4.

6. Floyd writes: "You will not make the intellectual sale of a new culture or any other major change to all the people throughout your organization until most of them have heard most members of management openly and consistently support the new ideas for quite some time." Floyd, *A Culture of Rapid Improvement: Creating and Sustaining an Engaged Workforce*, 186.

7. Another interesting point: "I have previously discussed the problem of confusing the tool or method with the goal. Mass generic training is a very common indicator that this may be occurring." Floyd, *A Culture of Rapid Improvement: Creating and Sustaining an Engaged Workforce*, 88.

Chapter 17

1. Edgar Schein, one of the gurus of culture change and "Organization Development," notes that it is a conceptual error to separate diagnosis from intervention, because one cannot make an adequate diagnosis without intervening. See Edgar Schein, "Kurt Lewin's Change Theory in the Field and in the Classroom: Notes Toward a Model of Managed Learning," invited paper for a special issue of *Systems Practice* (March 1995), 12–13.

2. See also Newbold, *Project Management in the Fast Lane*, chap. 15 entitled "Throughput: *Ichiban*."

Chapter 19

1. For example, "The person assigned by the performing organization to achieve the project objectives." *A Guide to the Project Management Body of Knowledge*, 369.
2. Toyota routinely helps their suppliers or teaches them about the Toyota Production System. They believe that any advantage their competitors gain is far offset by the benefits to Toyota.

Afterword

1. My answers:
    1: False. Changing and communicating fundamental ways in which people work are rarely easy.
    2: False. It takes experience as well. The cheapest, lowest-risk way to get experience is usually by being mentored by someone who has done it before. Learn from their mistakes.
    3: False. Detailed resource modeling can be appropriate, but it can also slow your progress toward the biggest benefits of PPM.
    4: Usually false. Don't think you will be able to flip a switch and have the new system in place. On the other hand, sometimes implementation speed is essential.
    5: False. The hard part is causing the right behavior changes. Tools can enable them, but they seldom cause them. Sometimes tools are subverted to support the old behaviors. Sometimes they actually cause the wrong behaviors.
    6: False.
    7: False.
    8: False. Focus on your work, give average durations, and if something takes longer get over it.
    9: False.

10: False. There are many new things; not with all the components, but certainly with the ways in which they are combined.

11: False. You and your colleagues have to solve your problems. Critical chain and PPM concepts can help.

12: False. The best workers are those who don't have to multitask.

13: False. If you expect to consume it all, chances are you will. If you expect to go as quickly as possible, that may happen too.

14: False. If you stop multitasking, all your work will benefit.

Appendix B

1. See, for example, J. Cabanis-Brewin, "So . . . So What?? Debate Over CCPM Gets a Verbal Shrug from TOC Guru Goldratt," PM Network 13 (December 1999), no. 12, 49–52.

2. Contrast this with the Zone of Reconciliation shown in figure 5.2.

3. In further discussions in this appendix we refer to "senior leadership" or "SL" when, depending on the situation, we may be talking about some combination of senior leadership, marketing, and the customer.

4. See the discussion on Duck Farming in Chapter 5.

INDEX

NOTE: Page references in *italics* refer to tables and figures.

measurement *(continued)*
  of rollout success, 225–231, *226*
  short-term, 135–138, 136, *136*
merge bias. *See* integration risk
Microsoft Project, for network building, 127
milestones, 5–6, *6*, 21–22, *23*, 23–26. *See also* critical chain scheduling; scheduling
  average duration *vs.*, 74, *74*
  defined, 261
  embedded safety time for, 78–79
  EPM system and, 34
  Imventure example, 77
  missed deadlines and, 26–28
  priorities contrasted with, 83–85
  rollout and, 216–221
Monte Carlo simulation, to buffer sizing, 104
Morton, William, 187
moving finish line, 27–28, 261
multi-project management, 143, 158
  communication for, 155–158, *157*
  fever chart, *157*
  pacing resource (drum resource) and, 148–151, *149, 150*
  pilot process and, 204
  program management, 153–155, *155*
  resource capacity management, 143–148, *144, 145*
  scheduling, practice, 151–153
multitasking, 9–10, 24–26, 261
  Confetti Factory exercise, 43–47, *44, 45*
  Mancala Game exercise, *48*, 48–50
  Multitasking Maelstrom, 49, 146, 152, 233, 261

negative feedback, as short-term measurement, 137–138
network building, 93–94, 121–122, 134
  analysis of network, 131–134
  initial considerations for, 122–123
  network, defined, 261
  preparation for, 125–127
  steps in process of, *124*
  task duration and, 127–131, *129*

network build team (NBT), 261. *See also* network building
  assembling, 125–127
  individual contributors (IC), 55, 129, 208, 260
  pilots and, 207, 208
  specialized expertise and, 132
Newbold, Rob, 36
New Game, 241–242, 246–257, *247, 256–257*
"new-old problem," 231
"no planning" loop, 64–66, *65*

Old Game, 241–246, *243, 256–257*
organization change. *See* change
outsourcing, 26, 253
overtime, planning for, 105
ownership, 8, 13, 31–34, 215
  change and, 180
  critical chain and buffer indicators, 118
  Imventure example, 87, *89*

pacing of projects, 148–153, 251
pacing resource (drum resource), 148–151, *149, 150*
Pareto Principle, 35–36
percent project completed, 111–114, *112, 114, 115*, 160
Percent Task Impact (PTI), 111, 118, 217, 262
personnel. *See* human resources
pharmaceutical industry, 17–18
planning, 3, 8, 14, 63–64, 68–69
  change and, 180
  critical chain and buffer indicators, 118
  culture change and, 40
  exponential levers and, 66–68
  Imventure example, 80–81, *89*
  "no planning" loop and, 64–66, *65*
portfolio-level tools, 94
PPM behaviors, 93–94, 159, 169–170, 240
  language of PPM and, 165–167, 238–239
  pilot process and, 204